HARDPRESS.NET
HOME OF HARD-TO-FIND BOOKS

The History of the Life and Death of His Most Serene Highness, Oliver, Late Lord Protector
by Samuel Carrington

Address:
HardPress
8345 NW 66TH ST #2561
MIAMI FL 33166-2626
USA
Email: info@hardpress.net

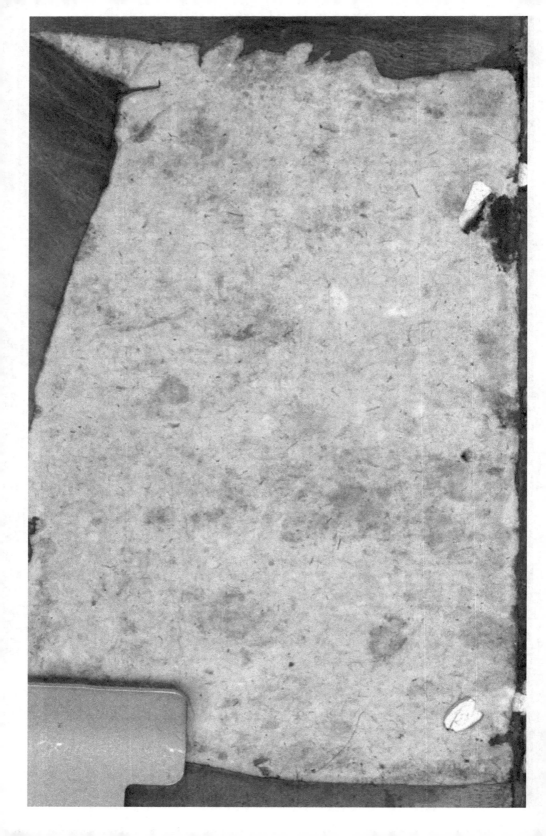

de

Brit.

108 rg

THE
HISTORY
OF THE
Life and Death

Of His most Serene Highness,

OLIVER,

Late Lord Protector.

Wherein, from his Cradle to his Tomb, are impartially transmitted to Posterity, the most weighty Transactions, Forreign or Domestique, that have happened in his Time, either in Matters of Law, Proceedings in Parliaments, or other Affairs in Church or State.

By *S. Carrington.*

Pax quæritur Bello.

London, Printed for *Nath. Brook*, at the Sign of the Angel in *Cornhill*, 1659.

To His most
SERENE HIGHNESS,
RICHARD,
Lord PROTECTOR
OF THE
Commonwealth of *England*,
Scotland, and *Ireland*, and the Dominions and Territories
thereunto belonging.

May it pleaſe Your Highneſs,

AS nothing can be preſented to the Potentates of the World of greater value,
then the Labours of Famous Hiſtorio-
graphers, who deſcribe to the life the
Examples of ſuch Eminent Perſonages as were
tranſcendent in preceding Ages; and may in their

Suc-

The Epiftle Dedicatory.

Succeffours beget both Emulation and Experience: fo fhall I not need to apprehend that this Hiftory (which in all humility I prefent unto Your Highnefs) will prove unacceptable, fince therein You may encounter with fuch a Model of all kinde of Vertues and Perfections, as I hope may take a deeper impreffion in Your Highneffes Breaft, in regard that it will be found, that Art herein is feconded by Nature. And whereas I am under the lafh of a fevere Caftigation for my prefumption, in profering this Hiftory to Your Review, as I acknowledge, when I ferioufly confider how You have attracted to Your Self that lively Pourtraiture of his Great Soul, that You appear the true Embleme both of his Vertues and Majefty.

May it pleafe Your moft Serene Highnefs, I cannot chufe but addrefs this prefent Oblation as to Your Self, fo in other Languages, to the reft of the Princes and Potentates of the Earth, I bequeath it unto pofterity, very humbly craving the favourable Protection of Your Highneffes Patronage. Nor durft I publifh fo glorious a Work to the World, before I had craved Your Highneffes pardon for my Rafhnefs, in adventuring to trace thofe Vigorous Lineaments in the Alexander, whom Your Highnefs fo well refembleth, and in whom your Highnefs beareth fo great a part. Moreover, as a fole Apelles could onely be capable of fo great an Enterprize, fo it will be altogether unneceffary for me to endeavour the Defcription of that Pourtraiture, which fo evidently

dently

The Epistle Dedicatory.

dently is manifested to all the World, both in Your Highnesses Person and Actions : Wherefore, my Lord, I must needs confess , that Your Highness is the true Original, and mine onely relating to the Out-side of so Great and unalterable an Albionist. The truth is, I finde not in my self ability to express the Real Worth of His Accomplishments, and Hardy Features, accompanied with that Vivacity and Lustre , which secret Mystery lyeth onely in the Hand of that great Master of Nature, and Extant in that very Personage, whose Simile is hardly this Day to be found in the whole Universe, except in Your Inimitable Self. Nor doth Art or Humane frailty allow so much to be in the Possession of the best men. Therefore those who go about to Pourtraict such like Incomparable Personages, cannot avoid one of those extremities, which Painters run into when they go about to represent the Sun ; who either place themselves at so great a distance, as that they can onely discover an inefficatious and feeble Reflections of its Beams ; or approach so neer unto it, as that being dazled with its Resplendency, and overcome with its Heat, they are bereaved of their Senses, and retain onely their Hearts at liberty to adore and admire that powerful Hand, which formed so glorious a Creature. To the like Non plus am I reduced, who rashly ascend to the very summit of the Throne of Honour , thence to contemplate his late Highness Person, surrounded by so glorious a Resplendency as no eyes are able to behold, nor to be comprehended by the mindes of men ; so

A 3

that

The Epistle Dedicatory.

that I must needs sink under the burthen, and
content my self with the Poets Expression,
———— Inopem me copia fecit.

In which extasie all my Senses being surprized,
my Heart is onely left free to admire, and my
Tongue to plead Excuses, and offer up good Wishes,
which I most humbly Dedicate and Devote unto
Your most Serene Highness. Nor could the
Heavens have ever established a more fitting Personage, to bear a share in, or inclination unto this
Work, then Your Highness, as well as to defend
it from Envy it self. And if so be History be
a second Life, Your Highness may judge by the
black Attempts which threatned Your Glorious
Father, how this work will be assailed; and how
many Enemies its Authour must resolve to enter into the Lists withall: their Rage being
thereby renewed and augmented, by their perceiving that the Tomb hath onely bereaved us of
the least part of this Great Heroe. And how
malicious soever their Envy may appear in such
Stories which possibly may be written in Contra-
diction hereof; it will onely publish from Truth
it self, to the World; their inveterate Spleen,
which can never pierce through the bright Rayes
of his Innocent and Glorious Actions.

Moreover, whereas the Divine Providence hath
so often and miraculously preserved the first life
of his late Highness, against the Attempts both
of men and monsters; Your most Serene Highness is also engaged, as well by Imitation, as
by the Interest of Your Care and Royal Dignity,

to

to watch over the Preservation of his second
Life, which is in Your Highness by so Lawful
a Succession, as is devolved upon Your Self.
The Glorious Course whereof I resolve to track
from this very moment; that I may the better
publish the Historical Transactions thereof in
five other Languages, which during my Travels
I have acquired. In which also I intend to publish
this present History, the French being already perfected and fit for the Press: His great Soul expecting proportionable Honours to its Dignity;
and his vaste Minde requiring numberless Ele-
gies, which may remain as so many living Monuments, not to be defaced by Times Violence nor
Envy. But I press this Subject too home to Your
Highness, since You bear so great a share therein, and my self dare attribute so little of it to
my own incapacity, of compassing so great an
undertaking.

Wherefore, I shall onely hereby endeavour to
attract others, and to shew them the Borders
and Coast of that vaste Sea into which they
ought to lanch: so that like to a Forelorn Hope,
I shall onely first mount the Breach, and by diverse Languages animate all the Trumpets of
Fame, to Celebrate the Glory of his late Highness, in those parts of the World, where I have
conversed for the space of sixteen or eighteen
years past. Hoping for the future to write the
Heroick Actions of this Nation in unexpugna-
ble Characters, to leave unto Posterity (as an
eye witness) the Rehearsal of those Victories

which

The Epistle Dedicatory.

which Heaven shall bestow on England , under Your Glorious Goverment ; that so I may the better satisfie my Zeal and Fidelity to Your Highness , and approve my self to be

Your Highnesses

most Humble, most Obedient, most Faithful Servant, and Loyal Subject.

S. Carrington.

The

The Preface.

Courteous Reader,

THat which I do here intend to present you with all, is, the Life and Death of *Oliver Cromwel*, late Lord Protector of the Commonwealth of *England*; that Grand Personage, whose Conduct and Fortune all the world doth admire; and who in the space of ten years time, did accomplish the work of a whole Age: nay more, he perfected the work of future Ages; having settled *England* on such good Foundations, that if she continues to build thereon, she may expect to produce second *Edwards*, and second *Henries*.

This Illustrious Personages life is presented unto you in three several Scenes; First, you will finde him Dormant, like unto *David* midst his Flocks, untill the Troubles of his Country awake him.
And

And that the Almighty was pleased to call upon him to appeale them, as well as to encreafe his glory, you may reflect upon the courfe and progrefs of his valour; by which being elevated almoſt to the fublimeſt pitch of his Grandeur, he was left to act more abfolutely according to his own prudence, and was enforced to lay hands on the Reins of the moſt confuſed State that ever was.

Where you will finde his late Highnefs demeaning himſelf like unto a well refolved skillful Pilot in a Veffel toffed and tumbled by a tempeſt, beſtirring himſelf amidſt the contrarieſt of Winds, and wifely and dexterouſly avoiding thofe Rocks, Shelves, and Quickfands, which threatned *England* with a fecond Shipwrack. This his fage conduct being the more to be admired, in that as then he had but a limited Power, although the whole was due to his dexterity and prudence; yet each one thought they had as great a fhare as himſelf in the Sovereign Power, which as they fuppofed they had acquired by the Pen or the Sword; either In the Army or in the Parliament: fo that all this great Politician

tician could as then do, was to reconcile those several Opinions then in agitation, and to suffer himself to be swayed
by the current of those windes and
streams which he was neither willing nor
well able to withstand at that time.

Now as there is nothing more dangerous in States then great and sudden
changes, so nothing more difficult to be
managed ; and this being the Masterpiece which a Politician hath to act, this
ensuing History will discover unto us the
chief and several Motions, Turnings,
Windings, and Settling of the same.

His late Highness like unto an expert
Physician, was first put to read the Tem-
perment of *England*, her former way
and manner of actings, before the Current of her Humors, and the Symptomes
of all the Evils and Malignities which
threatned her. He likewise reflected on
the Body Politick, which he found as
well as the Humane had its Replenish-
ments, and Evacuations, and Crisis ;
and then observed that as well in the one
as the other, those sudedn changes which
happen are either Destructive or Salutary. He observed that these Bodies nourished

rished Choller as well as other Humors; and thence deemed War to be the best *Rubarb* to purge them, least otherwise they might evacuate of themselves. Moreover, he observed these Humors were subject to grow sharp and to rebell, and that they oftentimes caused such violent and hot fits, as that without the assistance of an expert and accomplished Physician, death was like to ensue; or which is worst, most violent languishing and intollerable diseases. So that the thing which is most to be admired at in the conduct of this grand Politician, is, that he could governe a People, and procure a perfect Union and Tranquillity amidst three Nations, whose mindes were agitated by several Opinions, and whereby they are continually stirred against each other; no motion transporting men more impetuously towards civil Dissentions, then those which arise from the several Professions in Religion. For besides the chief Religions profest in these three Nations, *viz.* that of *Geneva,* the Protestant, the Episcopal, and some Roman Catholicks, there are sprung up throughout all *England,* an infinite number
ber

ber of other Sectaries, which like unto
so many *Hidra's*, did seem to issue forth
from each others neck; and whereby the
mindes of men were so discomposed and
hurried away into such violent Enthusi-
asmes, as they stood in need of a good
Guide to conduct and refrain them from a
total precipitation. And as it would be
a difficult task to give you the several
Denominations, Derivations, and Off-
springs of all these several Schismaticks,
I shall therefore pass them by as being
numberless.

Wherefore, if we acknowledge as it
is most assuredly true, that Religion is the
chief principal part which doth most of
all contribute to the well ordering, quiet, and peaceable settling and Governing
of a People; we may easily judge that
his late Highness the Lord Protector
stood in need of more then ordinary Sagacity, Prudence, and Conduct,
to procure that Tranquillity, Plenty, and
Splendour to *England*, wherein he left
it; and the which without example, is
hardly to be found in all the other parts
of *Europe*.

But to come nearer home, to my own
enter-

enterprize, the Life of an Historian is the Life of History; and his truth the most proper Preface to it. Thus much I can safely write for my self, that I have entertained no design beyond Truth; as I have not made this History subservient either to Flattery or Interest: I question not but the prejudice of some may go about to detect, but I am so confident of my own integrity, as to believe, no person can forme a truer Relation of the late disturbed Affairs of these Nations. I acknowledge where Originals have failed me, and must do others, I have conformed to Copies; but of so near extraction, as that they are but once removed from their Fountain.

I being so truly acquainted, my knowledge so strongly established to trace this History, as to discerne how to write, so also for the credit of my laborious Industry, I can affirme, That my Information was not without near approaches, as I continually conversed with the most principal Instruments in these admirable Transactions, persons Unbiased, that had certain and full Intelligence of the highest emergences, whether Forreign or Do-

Domeſtick. If I have been but as judicious and clear-ſighted to perceive and write, as I have been honeſtly unconcerned to tranſmit this Hiſtory to poſterity, I ſhall not need to fear but ſtand ſecure againſt the moſt malicious, or otherwiſe impertinent Imputations. Having thus diſcharged my Conſcience in theſe my honeſt endeavours, I have no more to write, but to bid thee read, and then cenſure Impartially. Farewell.

Thine,

S. C.

The Poſtſcript.

Reader, Be pleaſed to take notice that this Hiſtory is Tranſlating into five other Languages; it is in French ready for the Preſs: the other Tranſlations for other parts of the World being in ſuch forwardneſs, as that they will be ſpeedily extant.

An

An Advertisement.

Courteous Reader,

BE pleafed to take notice, that in the Page 195. feven lines before that never till now publifhed, an Incomparable Poem of the Eng-lifh *Virgil* of our times, Mr. *Edmund Waller,* on General *Mountagne's* wonderful Victory at Sea over the Spaniards, at *Sancta Cruze*, that in the Printing this efcaped, for *fhaming* read *fub-lime :* for other leffer Miftakes , the expedition of the Prefs may obtain thy excufe.

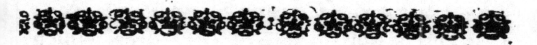

THE
HISTORY
Of his *Highneſs*
OLIVER,
The late
Lord-Protector,
From his Cradle to his Tomb.

The Introduction.

F thoſe Writers who pen the Hiſtories of great **Men**, had the ſame
advantage as **Painters** have, who
oblige thoſe whom they are to
Portraict, to ſeat themſelves in
h. a poſture, as they may beſt conſider and
ge of them, who do chooſe their Lights, and
reby diſcover moſt apparently the moſt de-
licate

C

licate and neateſt feature of the Faces, which they are to repreſent; I might hope to give unto the publick and to Poſterity a perfect Reſemblance of his late Highneſs the Lord Protector of *England*, although I ſhould meet with a great deal of difficulty in the well applying of the Colours, and to make choice of ſuch exquiſite Ones to trace the Footſteps of ſo glorious a Life. True it is, that the Soul is not viſible, as Mens Bodies are; for as it hath its Origine from Heaven, we muſt of neceſſity aſcend up thither, and enter into the Councels of the Almighty, to obſerve thoſe Lights and Inſpirations which he gives unto thoſe perſons whom his Divine Providence doth make choice of to command here on Earth, and thoſe deſigns which he doth frame in theſe great Souls, for the encreaſe of his Glory, and for our Peace and Tranquillity. So that our Ignorance doth oblige us herein to immitate the modeſty and good behaviour of Painters, who inſtead of a beautifull nakedneſs, render it to our view wrapt up in fine Linnen, and not diſcovering unto us the Brain, whence the ſeverall motions of the Body do proceed, they only ſet before our eyes a dumb Image without Motion, and ſome few Phyſionomical Marks, which do help us to gueſs who the party is they intend to repreſent unto us.

My intent is, to give you a rough Draught of this moſt excellent Perſonage, whoſe Actions are ſo glorious and ſurpaſſingly winning in themſelves, as that we ſhall only need to enter

upon

on a Relation of them, and so insensibly come
eat a Naturall Panegyrick, much like unto
ose exquisite Beauties, the advantages where-
we so much the more lessen, and detract from,
y how much the more we go about to embel-
sh them, with Ornaments and Cloathing; so
nat the Resplendency of my Subject it self
vill spare me the labour of making a long In-
roduction, and the vastness of its Renown saves
ne the care I ought to have taken in duly prepa-
ing the Readers Mind to conceive worthily of
his my *H E R O E*, and to have begot in them
a Love and Esteem of his Person.

His late Highness was born in the Town of
Huntington, the chief of the Shire, which bear-
eth the same Name, of a Noble Parentage, be-
ing descended from the Ancient and Illustrious
Family of the *Williams's*, of the County of
Glamorgan, which Name in the Reign of King
Henry the Eighth, was changed into that of
Cromwell, as will appear by the ensuing History. *His High-*
His Parents left him not much Wealth, but cau- *ness Birth*
sed him to be educated in the University of *and Paren-*
Cambridge; where, as it is reported, a publick *tage.*
Representation being to be performed, he that
was to represent the Kings part, falling sick, this
out *Cromwell* was said to have taken the Part
upon Himself, and so well imployed the little
time he had to get it by Heart, as it seemed, that *Lingua the*
it was Infused into him, and whereby he repre- *Combate*
sented a King with so much Grace and Majesty, *of the*
as if that Estate had been naturall unto him: *Senate.*
And truly thus much may be averred, that his

Soul comprehended all those Seeds and Foundations of such Vertues, as do usually render a Person capable to govern others.

His excellent qualifications.

Having finished his course of Study at the University, when he had perfectly acquired unto himself the Latine Tongue (which Language, as all men know, he made use of to treat with Strangers) His Parents designed him to the Study of the Civil Law, which is the Foundation of the Politicks: It being very requisite that he who was Ordained to give Law to three Kingdomes, and to the whole Sea besides, should have a smack of the Law, and chiefly of those which were the most Essentiall and Universall; for he dived not over deep into this Study, but rather chose to run a Course in all the rest of the Sciences, and chiefly in the Mathematicks, wherein he excelled, as likewise he may be justly said to have yeilded to no Gentleman whatsoever in the knowledge of the rest of the Arts and Sciences. But to keep more close to our History.

His Fortune and Rise did commence by those very means which by degrees elevated him to the Supream pitch of Grandeur. The conjuncture of Affairs brought him on the Stage, His Valour raised him up, and the Politick part taking the upper Hand as belonging to Her by Birth-right, Crowned him with all those Blisses which both the former and latter could justly discern.

Wherefore the Disorders of *England* and *Scotland* being not possible to be appeased without

out the intervening of a Parliament, there was one summoned in the year 1641. in which the late Protector affisted in the quality of a Burgess, for the Town of *Cambridge*, one of the most famous Universities of *England*, who could not fail in making so good a Choice, and so worthy of such Eminent persons as themselves, verst in all Sciences and Profound Knowledge. Things growing past an amicable reconciliation between the King and the Parliament, after severall and infinite Treaties and Proposalls; the last Reason both of the one and the other terminated in the loud Volleys of Canons, each Partie took the Field, and those Parliament Men who were minded to engage in the War, did with a generall consent and approbation obtain leave to suspend their Imployment in the House whereunto they were called, To maintain the Liberties of Parliament with the points of their Swords; His late Highness was none of the last that profered his Service to the Parliament, and the better to witness his Passion and Zeal to the Cause, he raised a Troop of Horse at his own costs and Charges. The esteem he had in the House, and he value which the County of *Essex* put upon his Person, obliged the Parliament to grant him a Commission to levy as many men as he ould, that so he might make up a compleat egiment : And as he was Burgess of the own of *Cambridge*, so his first care was to se e that place for the Parliament, although he et with great Obstacles therein, and the Rea son

the first Engagement.

son likewise was very harsh, it being the Month of *January*, the very heart of the Winter. Now you are to note, that the Universities of *Oxford* and *Cambridge* were the first of all the Towns in *England* which declared themselves for the King, and the last which acknowledged the new established Authority; by reason they were filled with persons designed to possess those Church Goods which were in the Kings Donation, besides which the Parliament detesting their Commissions, was resolved to reduce and reform them.

The Treasure of the University failed on.

His late Highness having notice that all the Colledges were making a Stock and Assembly of all their Plate, and of what ready monies they had, to send it unto the King, all which amounted unto a very considerabe Sum, went suddenly to *Cambridge*, and seized all that Treasure just as it was ready to be sent away unto *Oxford*: And as he was upon this Expedition, he signallized himself far more by another Action; Sir *Thomas Comes* who was newly made Sheriff of *Hertford* Shire, had received Orders from the King, to publish a Proclamation, by which the County of *Kent*, and all its Adherents were proclaimed Traytors: His late Highness surprised him in the very Action on a Market-day, in the Town of St. *Albons*, and having seized the said Knight, he sent him up to the Parliament.

And not long afterwards he very oportunely assembled all the Forces of the County of *Cambridge*, & exhorted the Neighbouring Counties of *Suffolk*, *Norfolk*, and *Essex*, to send him their

their Aydes to oppose the Lord *Capell*, who was to have been seconded by Prince *Rupert*, and should have seized *Cambridge*, and thereby have impeded the association of the united Counties about *London*, which were the only Bulwark and Defence of that great City, wherein the Sinews of War did consist, and by whose resolutions and proceedings the rest of the Kingdome was then governed; His Highness diligence and vigilancy at that time, brake the Neck of that Design, and forced the Lord *Capell*, and Prince *Rupert* to direct their Thoughts another way. In the beginning of the Month of *March*, next ensuing, his late Highness having compleated a Regiment of Horse to the full number of a thousand Men, marched with great diligence into the County of *Suffolk*, on the advice which he had received of a great Confederacy which was there hatching between the Nobility of the Kings Party who were assembled in a considerable Town, called *Lowerstoft*; whom he so unsuspectedly surprised, as that he became Master of the place without the fiering of one Gun; He took Prisoners Sir *Thomas Barker*, Sir *John Pettus* his Brother, Mr. *Knevet*, *Catlines Hammond*, *Cory Turrill*, *Preston*, and above twenty other Persons of Note. He likewise there took severall parcels of Armes and Ammunitions and other War-like Equipages, sufficient to have armed a considerable Party, and had not his Highness made use of his accustomed Prudence, and his usual Activity in this Conjuncture, he had met with a great deal of difficulty on this sad

count,

count, and the whole Country had run a danger to
have been loft: feverall perfons of Quality, and
divers Noble men hourly flocking to that Ran-
dezvous ; This Service was moft feafonably
rendred to the Parliament, and the Kings Party
both in *Suffolk* and *Norfolk*, were thereby totally difheartned and difcouraged.
     The Spring being advanced, and the Seafon
permitting the framing of greater Defigns, and
taking of longer Marches, his Highnefs having
well fetled the Peace and Tranquillity of the af-
fociated Counties ; which (as we have fayd) ferved as a Bulwark to the Parliament, his Mind
and his Valour requiring a fpace of Ground as
vaft as its Activity, he raifed a Body of an Army
and that a very confiderable one, being compo-
fed of fuch zealous perfons as had already been
charmed with his Conduct, and being attracted
by his Reputation, did voluntarily come in unto him to ferve with, and under him in the
Caufe of Religion ; He thus Marched into *Lin-
colnfhire,*with a Refolution to affift thofe Forces
which lay about *Newark*, one of the ftrongeft
places which held out as then for the King, into
which the greateft part of the Gentry of *Lin-
colnfhire* had retired themfelves, and where there
was a good Garifon commanded by Officers,
who had ferved their Apprentifhips in the Military Art beyond the Seas ; fo that they fetcht
in vaft Contributions out of the Neighbouring
Counties, and made Inroads to the very Gates
of *Lincoln* : And his Highnefs being now at the
Head of a Regiment of Horfe, in his paffage
                                        through

through *Huntingtonshire* was willing to deliver his Native Country from those Disorders which two contrary Parties do usually cause and commit being in one thing he therefore disarmed all those who were hot affectioned to the Parliament, by which means he so enlarged and augmented his Troops that he had gotten two thousand Men together, and before he came neer *Newark*, he received another re-inforcement of Horse, which was sent him by Captain *Hotham*, as also some other Troops which were sent him from *Lincolne* insomuch that he thus framed a sufficient considerable Body of an Army for that time. He no sooner was come nigh to *Newark*, but that he signallized himself by an Action which was the more glorious, by how much the less it was expected nor foreseen; Captain *Wray*, having so inconsideratly placed himself with his *Lincolne* Horse, too nigh *Newark*, was in the Night set upon by the Garrison, which made a great Sally, and surrounded and took all his Men, the Alarm comming hot to his late Highness Quarters, he forthwith repaired to the place where the Fight was, it being then about ten of the Clock in the Night, relieved the said Captain *Wray*, and took three whole Companies of the Enemy, killed the rest on the place, and made good his Retreat, by Favour of the dark Night.

After which, having blocked up the place, he received those Sallies which were made by the Besieged, with so much Courage and Vigilancy, as that he alwaies came off with advantage, sometimes

A remarkable expedition.

sometimes forcing the Enemies into their very Works, and sometimes cutting them in pieces, insomuch that he never returned unto the Camp but he was laden either with Prisoners, Spoyles or Colours, and that he might neglect no occasion for to give a testimony of his Prudence and Activity, he also scouted abroad into the Country with his Horse, and neer unto *Grantham* he defeated a strong Party which came forth of *Newark*, with a handful of Men, onely since which, the World did take notice that there was somewhat more then ordinary in the person of his late Highness : And not long after he also defeated part of the Lord of *Newcastles* Army, which came to relieve *Newark*, setting upon them in their Quarters betwixt *Grantham* and *Newark*, where he took one hundred Horses, forty Prisoners, and killed severall on the place. And should I particularlize all his late Highness's memorable Actions, during these English Civill Wars, I must of necessity compile a whole Volume thereof, since nothing worth the taking notice of ever hapned in which he was not a Sharer, and wherein he was not alwaies one of the foremost : wherfore I shall only insist upon two chief Actions which were of so great Importance, that the decision of the whole War depended thereon, and wherin the Valour of his late Highness may justly claim the greatest, if not the sole share. Two of the Parliaments Armies, the one commanded by the Lord *Fairfax*, and the other by the Lord *Manchester*, being united to the Scotch Army

their

their Confederates, Commanded by the Earl of *Livin*, had joyntly besieged the City of *York*, the Metropolis of that County, and whereof the Earl of *Newcastle* was Governour for the King, who over and above his Garison which was very strong, had also a brave and gallant Army, Prince *Rupert* was sent by the King to raise that Siege, with such considerable Forces, as being joyned to those of the Earl of *Newcastle*, did well nigh equallize the Parliaments in number. The three Parliament Generals did immediatly raise the Siege to encounter Prince *Rupert*, and the Earl of *Newcastle*, drew forth also his Forces out of the Town, and both Armies being drawn up in Battrell-Array upon *Marston* Moore, they both fought with a great deal of Fury, Animosity, and hopes of Victory, which at first seemed to incline to the Kings Part, the right Wing of the Parliaments Forces Commanded by the Lord *Fairfax*, having the disadvantage of the Ground, was over-whelmed by the left Wing of the Kings Party, who routed and defeated it: But his late Highness (who as then was stiled but a Colonel) whose after Appellations I shall observe by degrees, which Fortune advanced him to) who commanded the left Wing, and had not the least advantage of the Ground, did so violently set upon the right Wing of the Kings Party, as that he brake in peeces Prince *Ruperts* best Regiments, and forced them not only to give way, but to turn their Backs, and suffering only some part of his Men to pursue the Enemy, he with the rest made half a turn about

and

and charged the Enemies main Battell in the
Rear so vigorously, as that putting Life again in
to the Lord *Fairfax's* Souldiers, he constrained
them to face about, and thereby so well restor
red the Success of the Battell, as that he obtain,
ed and Entire and compleat Victory. Two Ge
nerals of the Enemies, and some of the best
mounted of their Officers only making their es-
capes by their Horses good heels; and this Battell was accounted the greatest that ever was
fought during these last Wars.

His High-
ness admi-
rable ma-
nagement
of the Bat-
tell at
Naseby.

The same thing likewise hapned in the famous Battell of *Naseby*, near unto *Northampton*,
when as his late Highness arriving in the Camp
but on the Evening before the Fight gave
such encouragement and joy to the whole Army, by reason of his so suddain and unexpected
Arivall from so great a distance of place, as that
it presaged an undoubted Victory. The left
Wing of the Parliaments Army was quite over
borne; General *Ireton* his late Highness Son-in-
Law, and who afterward governed *Ireland* in the
Quality of Lord Deputy, with as much Prudence
and Conduct as he shewd Valour and Deserts to
merit so considerable an Imployment, being
the second Person of the Common-wealth,
was carried off from the Field by two Wounds
he received, and was taken Prisoner, but was
relieved again, and Prince *Rupert* pursued his
Victory with as much vigour and hopes to gain
the Battell, as if the day had been his own: But
his late Highness on his side defeating that
Wing which was oposite to him, charged them
with

with such force and Courage, as that he made the Victory dubious, and so it continued for a good while, neither inclining to the one side, nor the other, till at last the Kings Horse falling a running, left their Foot to shift for themselves, which were all cut in pieces and taken Prisoners, all the Canon & Baggage was likewise taken, of a considerable value; there was also found a Cabinet of the Kings with his Papers of great Importance : The royall Standard, and one hundred Colours beside were brought off, and his late Highness having pursed the Kings Horse as long as he listed, at length returned to the Camp with a great number of Prisoners. Should I go about to number up the severall places of consequence which this Conquerour hath taken, either by force or by Capitulations, I should fill up a whole Volume with the Names of Towns and Fortresses alone; besides intending hereby only to give you a Perspective of his glorious Life : I will only instance in those worthy Actions of his, whereby the Fortunes of the Wars did decide the possession of three Kingdomes.

Nor may we omit to reckon amongst the rest of his Heroick Atchievements, the Victory which he obtained by *Preston* in *Lancashire*, over Duke *Hamilton*, and Sir *Marmaduke Langdale*, whose united Forces amounted unto 25000, his late Highness having not above 10000 at most, notwithstanding which inequallity of Forces he gave them Battell, and entirely routed that

The Victory of *Preston* in *Lancashire*.

puissant

puissant Army, killing 3000 Scotch upon the place, and taking 9000 Prisoners, chasing the remaining Forces to *Warrington* about 20 Miles from the place where the Battell was fought, and taking Duke *Hamilton* Prisoner, at a place called *Uttoxeter*, whither he was retired with 3000 Horse, as also Sir *Marmaduke Langdale*, the one by my Lord *Grey*, and Colonel *White*, and the other by Captain *Widmerpoole*, so that but few Scotch returned to their own Country, to cary back the News of so prodigious a Defeat.

The Monarchiall Government changed into a Common Wealth.

NO sooner were the Civill Wars of *England* terminated by the discomfiture of all the Kings Armies, the taking of his own Person, and by his death, but the Parliament by a solemn Vote and Ordinance, changed the Monarchiall Government into a Common-wealth. The Kingdome of *Ireland* was the first that witnessed a discontent of this Change, and all the severall Parties there uniting themselves on the News of this Change, they owned the late Kings Son, and joyned all their Forces against the Interest of the Common-wealth, and on a suddain became so powerfull and formidable, as that the chief Places in those Parts submitted to their obedience, *Dublin* only, and *London Derry* excepted, the first whereof was immediatly besieged by an Army of 22000 Men, Commanded by the Marquis of *Ormond*, and the other by a considerable Party, the Natives of the Country. The

The Royallists were as yet in possession of the
Isles of *Jersey* and *Man*, which places, although
they were adjacent unto *England*, yet they only
stood them in stead for a retreat to some Ships,
which robbed up and down the Seas in those
Parts: Nor were the Irish Businesses there arrived at the height of perfection, whereas they began to decline: for 2000 Horse and Foot which
the Parliament sent into *Ireland*, as the forerunner only of a more considerable Body being safely landed at *Dublin*, joyned themselves unto
the Garison, and unto the rest of the Forces
which could be got together in a Body, which
in all amounted not unto above 9000 Men, and
who joyntly made so generall and vigorous a
Sally upon the Marquis of *Ormond* (which Sally was so well ordered by the Prudence of Colonel *Michael Jones*, and so well encouraged and
led on by his Prudence and Valour together)
as that they forced the Marquis to quit the
Siege, and so well prosecuted the point of their
Victory, as that they cut all the said Marquises
Troops in pieces, who with much ado saved
himself; there were slain in the Combat and
pursuit about 2000 Men, as many were taken
Prisoners, and all the Ammunition of War, with
the Baggage and Ordnance were likewise left
behind as a Prey to the Besieged.

And the better to advance this generall Defeat, and to cause these puissant Confederates
the sooner to run into their Ruine, who a little
before promised themselves no less then the
Conquest

Forces sent into Ireland.

General Cromwell goes for Ireland, and arrives there in August, 1649.

Conquest of the three Kingdomes; *Oliver Cromwell* being by the Common-wealth nominated *Governour* of *Ireland*, took footing at *Dublin* with an Army furnished with all Necessaries requisite toward the Crowning of an Undertaking, which already had so happy and successfull a beginning.

But General *Cromwell* having in vain sought for the Enemies, who by these additionall Forces were forced to take Sanctuary in the best places and Fortresses of the Country, at length besieged *Drogedah*, one of the best and considerablest places in all *Ireland*, defended by so strong a Garrison as it might well have framed a little Army, and was commanded by such Officers as had been signallized beyond the Seas, whose numbers were so exceeding great, as that several of them bare Armes only as private Souldiers. There was no time spent in the framing of a Siege, or in the opening of Approaches, but each one minded the beating of the Iron whilst it was hot, and concluded that the Confederates ought not to be suffered to rally themselves, nor to unite in a Body again, wherefore a slight Breach being made, the Orders were given out for a generall Assault, but the Walls were lined with so many and so good Men chiefly in those places where the Assault was to be given, as that the solidst and gravest Officers of the Army did represent unto his Excellency the General, that there was no appearance at all to carry the place by force, but that it would be better to tire

Drogedah in Ireland besieged.

tyre and weary out the besieged by the length of a siege, during which the breach might be made the larger. But Generall *Cromwell*, whose prudence (as we have already observed) seconded his valour, did briskly answer them that he would goe and open the breach for them, and placing himselfe at the head of his Troops, caused the assault to be given, rendring this example of wisdome to all great Personages, that in Actions of important consequence neither Age, nor great Commands, or high Preferments, ought to hinder a General to be the first man to goe on upon an assault, since it must render them the most considerable, and raise them up to the highest pitch of honour and esteem.

Finally, after a sharp and bloody contest hand to hand, most obstinately maintained on all sides, the *English* forced their entrance, and the General went into the place pell mell with his Souldiers, at which time the ardour and heat of the victory did appear to correspond with his prudence, for though his generosity did oblige him to give quarter to those who had so well defended themselves, notwithstanding, deeming it fitting to make that place an example of terror unto the rest of the Towns which were garrisoned, and which might cost him too dear should they stand out as sturdily and obstinately as these did, he caused all those to be put to the sword who were found to be in Arms, & thus he sacrificed 3000

D *Irish,*

Irish unto the Ghosts of 10000 *English* whom they had massacred some years before. The taking of this place was followed by the surrender of several others, fear causing the weakest to yield; but those which were able to defend themselves were sold at dear rates. *Trim, Dundalke, Nury, Wexford, Rone, Bandonbridge* and *Kingsale* were subdued, this last being a very considerable passage, so likewise were several other places taken by the respective Commanders of the Common-wealth, at the self same time in the other parts of *Ireland,* and several parties of the Enemies field-Forces were likewise defeated by Sir *Charles Coot,* Collonel *Venables* and *Jones,* and the Lord *Broghill,* each of them signalizing themselves according to their accustomed valours, and the Lord *Broghill* having since made it appear in the managing of States affairs that he is as great a Politician as a Souldier. One would have imagined that the impetuous course of these victories should absolutely have quelled and abated the courage of the *Irish,* or that force and might would soon have reduced them to terms of reason, but they held out for a long time together in unaccessable places, in Woods and Bogges, over which none but the Natives both Horse and Men can passe without perishing, which doth manifest unto us, that the Conquest of that Island is not so easie at present, as it was formerly when *Henry* the second of *England* reduced it in one Winter, which, as certain Writers say, is almost in-

incredible: That so populous a Nation, so hardy, so well disciplined, so active and dexterous, should not so much as lift up a hand to defend themselves. But as the same writer saith, it is apparent that they were not accustomed to our manner or wayes of warring, nor to defend themselves against such kinde of weapons as were then used; however, if the Conquest was easie, the preservation was not found to be so, and cost farre dearer. True it is, that this last Conquest of that Nation was not so suddenly achieved, but those means which have been used to assure and preserve it, will give occasion unto our nephewes,——that this present age hath much profited by the faults and omissions of our Ancestors. Moreover, that fire which the Civil Warres had kindled in the *Britannick Islands*, was so violent, as that all the Sea which separates the Old World from the New, was not capable to hinder the Communication thereof even to their Colonies in *America*, for *Virginia* and the *Carybde* Islands refused to acknowledge the power of the Commonwealth, all those who inclined thereunto were either banished or executed, and despoyled of their goods, and however those Collonies could not subsist but by the Commerce of *England*, and that this Revolt did bring along with it their ruine, yet their obstinacy was such, as that they would neither yield to their own Interest nor Reason. Till at length the Common-Wealth sent a Fleet thither, under the

Command of Sir *George Askue,* who delivered
them out of their miseries, by ranging them
under the obedience of the Parliament. Meanwhile the Royallists Forces were very considerable at Sea, for Prince *Rupert* had a Fleet of
nine great Ships which served to shelter several other small ones, whereby the trade of *England* was much impeded and incommodated,
which obliged the Parliament to put forth a
most puissant Naval Army to Sea, fitted with
good Mariners, and all kinde of necessary war-
like Ammunitions. The sole brute of this Fleet
made all the Enemies Ships to run into their
several skulking holes like unto so many Conies,
and Prince *Rupert* being not strong enough to
encounter them, was forced to retire into
Kingsale Haven in *Ireland,* where he was immediately blocked up by the Parliaments Fleet,
whilest General *Cromwell* besieged both the
Port and Town by land, and Prince *Rupert* being forced to make a vertue of necessity, resolved to bear the brunt of all the *English* Fleet,
and so saved himself, leaving behinde him three
Ships, which by that occasion were taken, and
finally after several turnings and turmoilings,
he cast anchor at *Lisbone,* where he was protected by the King of *Portugal,* which caused
the rupture betwixt this Common-wealth and
that Crown, and all those mischiefs which ensued, as we hereafter shall rehearse.

　Meanwhile the Royallists in *Scotland* seeing
the Parliament was busied in *Ireland,* thought to
lay

lay hold on a fit opportunity to play their game, and to that purpose the Earle of *Montrosse* having landed in the North of *Scotland,* with some Forces he had raised in *Holland* and other parts, assembled the old Souldiers who had formerly served under him, and armed them with such Arms as he had brought from *Holland,* but before he could make a considerable body, he was defeated by the Presbyter Forces, taken, and hanged on a very high Gibbet, which is the last mark of infamy in that Countrey.

Within a while after, there was a Treaty commenced at *Breda,* between the *Scots* and their King, to install and re-establish him in that Kingdome, and in the others, according as Fortune should answer their designs and expectations ; and to this end, they deputed Ambassadors into *Spain, Italy, Denmarke, Sweden, Russia,* and into *Turkey,* and finally throughout all *Europe,* to demand relief, aid and assistance : But all their Embassies procured neither men nor money, only their Ambassadors were laden with Complements and good wishes in return, each others particular affairs not permitting them to do more.

All which gave unto the Common-wealth of *England,* not any great fears, but great jealousies, wherefore the better to be informed of the passages abroad, and the better to fortifie themselves by foraign Leagues and Alliances, Mr. *Dorislaus* a person full of knowledge and

con-

conduct, was sent in the quality of an Agent towards the States of the United Provinces, the chief drift of this Negotiation being to cement a good and firm understanding between the two Common-wealths. But scarce was he arrived at the *Hague,* when five or six disguised persons entred forcibly into his Chamber and massacred him. And whilest it seemed all things were a profound Calm in *England,* or that at least the course of the Enemies designs both at home and abroad, being sufficiently known to the State, on a suddain there sprang up the most formidable faction that ever was hatch'd since these last Warres : A certain number of persons who called themselves *Levellers,* whose pretenses were to render all mens goods and possessions alike, and truely this was a very plausible design, and might doubtlesse have met with as many Abettors as there are men in the world, who have no other possessions or Revenues, but their good will to obtaine them.

The chief of these Levellers was one *John Lilborn,* a man of a daring and attempting spirit, who could not remain quiet, but was altogether invincible, not to be moved by threats nor gained by the favour or presents of fortune, which were beneath the extent of his ambition, and a considerable part of the Army, siding with their Leader, they augmented in numbers as fast as the shortnesse of the time would permit, the confluence of such men as flattered

them-

themselves with such fond hopes, and who
promised themselves a revenge, and and establishment by a second Revolution and change.
But before all those who intended to have sided
with them could come up to them and unite in
one body, they were vigorously set upon by the
Lord *Fairfax*, at that time the Common-
wealths General, who defeated them at a place
called *Burford* in the County of *Oxford*, where
their Leader and the best part of his Souldiers
were taken, some of which were put to death
for example sake, and some others were banish'd, but the greatest part were pardoned, and
admitted into favour again.

As for their Leader *John Lilborne* being
brought up to *London*, he appeared before the
chief Officers and Judges of *London* and *Westminster*, the Lord Maior, Sheriffs, and divers
others, where he was not only accused of divers Martial Crimes, but also Politick ones, as
having been the Author of several scandalous
and defamatory Libells against the State, which
tended to render the Government odious, and
to beget a Mutiny in the people; however, he
so dexterously shifted himself of all these accu-
sations, as that the Judges declared him Not
guilty. Much about that very time, Mr. *Anthony
Ascham* a most judicious and accomplished
Gentleman, was Deputed and sent over in the
quality of an Agent to the King of *Spain*, and
arrived at the Port of *Sancta Maria* on the 5.
of *June* 1650, where being advertised that his

D 4   person

person was in danger, he was constrained to cause himself to be guarded to *Madrid,* where the next day after his arrival, as he was at Dinner, six men knocked at his Chamber doore, which was immediately opened unto them, and he rising from the Table to receive them, the first of the said parties stabbed him in the head with a Dagger, so that he fell down dead to the ground, and his Interpreter *Signior Riba* being not able to make his escape soon enough, was likewise stabbed in the belly; which being thus done, the Murderers would have saved themselves in the *Venetian* Ambassadors house, who refused them protection, whence they retired themselves into a Church, which in *Spain* is a Sanctuary which the Justice ought not to violate, whence however the King of *Spain* had them taken, and put into prison, one only excepted, who made an escape. Hence there arose a great contest betwixt the King and the Clergy, who complain'd that their priviledges had been infringed, and demanded that the Prisoners might be returned unto them: and on the other side, the Parliament of *England* pressed hard to have justice done on them, and though message upon message, instance upon instance were used therein, yet they took no effect. And lest it may seem that all these foraign Negotiations which we have here inserted, may be beyond my subject, however if they be considered as so many obstacles which Fortune opposed unto the vertue and

great-

greatness of his late Highness, you will find that the recitall of them will not be altogether useless, the rather since I have related them as succinctly as possibly: Besides, we may also look upon them as so many seeds sowen, to beget those warres which thereon ensued, and which were by the late Protector, rather by most glorious Treaties whereunto he was sought, or by most signal Victories which were obtain'd, and brought to a happy period, by which the blood of these two Agents, so cruelly murdered, were retaliated with use. But to go on to our History, the Treaty of *Breda* being absolutely concluded, and notwithstanding the great Antipathy and animosity between the Royallists and the Presbyterians, all their jealousies and grudges were seemingly reconciled, so that the *Scotch* wanted nothing to compleat their design, but to enjoy their Kings presence, who immediately coming to the *Hague*, went thence for *Schevelinge*, and embarqued himself for *Scotland* notwithstanding the dangers and perils of the Sea, which were very great, and the *English* Ships which had way-laid him to surprize him. As soon as he was landed in *Scotland*, the first thing they propounded unto their King was to take the solemn Oath, called the Covenant, that burning Torch which the Mother of *Paris* did see in her frenzies, that fatal fire which the *Scotch* believe descended from Heaven, and by which they at their pleasures kindle those warres where-

with

with they infett *England,* which Covenant as
we know was only a fuperftitious and warlike
Proteftation made in the prefence of God and
Men : *To maintain the purity of the Religion, to*
preferve the priviledges of Parliament, and the peo-
ple, and to re-eftablifh the King in his Anceftors
Throne.

But that which feemed fomewhat harfh and
rude to this Prince, was the terms wherein they
caufed him to take this Oath, quite contrary to
Phyfitians, who dip their Pills in Syrrops or
Sugar, to make them down the glibber, yet
thefe Politicians when the whole lay at the
ftake, it feems, troubled themfelves not much
with the wording of the thing ; for amongft
real friends indeed, there needs not many complements nor much complacence to be ufed.
Therefore the Churches of *Scotland* made their
King fwallow this reftorative in the following
Beverage, conftraining him to proteft, That
he renounced the finnes of his Fathers and his
own houfe, the Idolatry of his Mothers, and
that he would adhere unto Gods caufe in conformity to the Covenant, in the firm eftablifh-
ment of the Church Government, as it was expreffed in the Directory, for that publick wor-
fhip which is to be rendred to God, contained
in the Belief and Catechifm : And this Cup he
was forced to drink, that he might obtain his
Fathers Kingdome, which formalities were
more then requifite for to eftablifh that Prince
in the opinion of the prevailing party, which
was

was only then in a condition to help him. Howbeit the *English* knew very well to distinguish between these Artificial fictions, and the truth, for the Parliament of *England* being duely informed of the *Scots,* their designs and practises, thought it was high time to think of the best means to oppose them, and after several consultations upon this businesse, it was resolved that the Lord *Fairfax* should command the Army in chief, and with all speed march toward the North of *England.* But he most humbly thanked the Parliament, and like unto a second *Cincinatus,* retired himself from the Dictatorship to a Countrey-life, excusing himself for not serving them in that Expedition, upon his Indisposition at that time. The Renown of General *Cromwell's* feats of Arms, both as Governour and Conqueror of *Ireland,* admitted of no lesse Proposals, then to make him Generalissimo of the Common-wealths Armies, in the Lord *Fairfax* his stead: So that he came over again into *England,* whilest his hands were as yet warm, and was sent to give a check unto other Enemies in another Climate, and under another disguise, after he had settled and assured all the Conquests of *Ireland,* and had left the necessary and requisite Orders, conducing to a solid peace and establishment of those parts, with his sonne-in-Law *Henry Ireton,* so that he returned thence laden with Palms and Laurels, as Trophies of his worthy Acts in those parts. And scarce was he returned home, but he was en-

The Common-wealth prepares to war against the Scots.

His late Highness made Generalissimo of the Common-wealths Armies.

enforced to march towards those parts, whither the glory of Conquering a second Kingdome called upon him. Now the Scots, who by no means would make any outward shew of the grand designs which they were hatching, at the approach of the *English* Army on their Frontiers, seemed to be very much astonished; and the whole Countrey took the Allarum, moreover, the better to colour this their astonishment and seeming surprizal, they deputed a Messenger to Sir *Arthur Haslerigge,* as then Governour of *Newcastle,* upon the Borders of *England* and *Scotland,* to know the reason of that so suddain March of the *English* Army towards their Frontiers, whereunto they joyned several Manifesto's, setting forth the Contents of the Leagues and ample Treaties of union between the two Nations, and several other particulars, which served only to gain time, and to make the better preparations to receive their Enemies. At the same time of the *English* Armies advance towards the North, the Parliament set forth a Manifest accompanyed by another from the General, and chief Officers of the Army, whereby both the one and the others declared, *viz.* That the reasons which moved them to this great undertaking, was neither the support which they expected from the Arm of flesh, nor the consideration or vanity of former successes, nor the desire they had to compasse any of their own designs; But the true assurance they had, that their cause was just

before

A Manifest concerning the Scotch warre.

before God; reflecting on the foregoing Revolutions, and the successe which had followed them, not as the handy-work of Politick men, or of Humane force, but as the most eminent works of Providence, and the power of God, thereby to make his good will appear, and to shew his pleasure concerning those things which he had decreed in this world: That they were obliged, not to betray the cause wherein God had so evidently manifested himself, after which there was nothing more dear unto them then the preservation of those who feared the Lord, and who might greatly suffer either by being mistaken, or by not being capable to discern the true tye of a Generall Calamity, of which their Christian charity they hoped they had given sufficient proofs, at the last time, when they were in *Scotland* with this very Army, of which God was pleased to make use, for to break in pieces the power of those who oppressed the faithfull in those parts. But that the acknowledgements of so signal a favour, did but little appear in the Engagement which they had lately made with their new King, and that they had not proceeded like unto good Christians, in publishing that their Army was but an Army of Sectaries: However, that they doubted not, but that God would give them the grace to forgive them that calumny, and to that effect they beseeched him to be so good unto them, as to separate the Chaffe from the good Corn, concluding in like manner as they had begun,

The History of Oliver Lord Protector,
begun by a most solemn and terrible Impreca-
tion, beseeching that in testimony of the truth of
all these particulars, the great God of Heaven,
through his infinite mercy pardoning their fail-
ings and weaknesses, would judge betwixt them
when they should come to joyn in battle with
their Enemies. This Manifesto was sent from
the Generals quarters, as then at *Barwick*,
to the Metropolitan of *Scotland*, by a Trumpet,
whose eyes the *Scots* did blinde both going and
coming. Meanwhile the Army advanced as
farre as the Lord *Mordington's* Castle, on the 24
of *July*, 1650. and refreshed there three days,
on the 25. they advanced towards *Copperspeth*,
and the 26. they arrived at *Dunbar*, where the
Army received those Ammunitions wherewith
such Ships were laden, as were come thither on
purpose to observe the motions of the Army,
by reason that the Peasants had abandoned
their dwellings, not leaving so much as any
thing which might serve for refreshing. The
Army being somewhat refreshed at *Dunbar*,
marched toward *Haddington*, and the next day
understood, that the Enemies were disposed to
give them battle on a Heath called *Gladsmore*,
so that the *English* endeavoured to possesse
themselves of the place. But the *Scots* appeared not, whereupon it was resolved, that Major
General *Lambert*, and Colonel *Whalley* persons of an approved valour (and who have since
proved themselves as great Politicians as they
were great Commanders) should with 1400
Horse

Horse advance towards *Musclebrough*, to endeavour if possible to draw forth the Enemy, and to engage him to fight, whilest the rest of the Army marched up unto them. Whereupon there happened some slight skirmishes, but the *Scots* would not by any means be engaged in a general Combate; so that the *English* that night encamped hard by *Mustleborough*, from whence the *Scots* were but four miles distant, defended by a brest-work which they had drawn from *Edinborough* to *Leith*, and which was well nigh flanked all the way by the Canon of the last place; so that they were possessed of a very advantagious Port. The *English* being approached unto *Muscleborough* with a resolution to have set upon the Enemy in their works, found that it was a difficult matter to force their Line, and so were constrained to set down their Camp hard by that place all the day, to discover the countenance of the Enemy: But the desire they had to fight was somewhat abated by a great showre of rain, which continued all the day, and which did much incommodate them, by reason they had no shelter at all. On the 30. finding that they were put to it for want of Victuals, and the ground being so throughly soaked by the rain, as that it was farre more difficult to attempt the Enemy then before; the *English* retired to their former quarters; which begat heart in the *Scots* who sallyed out of their Lines, and fell so fiercely upon the Rearguard of the *English*, as that they put them into a kinde of disorder, but some Squadrons of Horse fronting in the Rear, and making good the ground, assured the March of the foot, and so vigorously continued their charge, as that they had like to have brought the businesse to a general Combate, had not the Commander in chief of the Scots Army caused a retreat to be sounded, that so they might bring their men into their Lines again, whither the English pursued them, fighting all the way with their Cavalry. In this Encounter, Major General *Lambert* ingaged so farre, as that he was hurt in the Arm with a Launce, and received another wound in the body, and once he was taken prisoner, but was rescued again by Lieutenant *Empson* of the Generals Regiment ; there were but few *English* killed, but farre more of the *Scotch,* and amongst them some persons of quality, several prisoners of theirs were also taken, as a Lievtenant Colonel, a Major, and some Captains. By which means the *English* recovered *Muscleborough* that night without being molested by the Enemy, but they were so disheartened for want of sleep, and so tyred by the dirty slabbery wayes, as that misdoubting least the enemy being aware thereof might give them an Alarum, that night they stood upon their guard, and accordingly they failed not betwixt three and four of the clock in the Morning, with fifteen Companies of choice Horse, commanded by Major General *Montgomery,* and Collonel *Straughton,* to

fall

fall into the *English* quarters with such a vehemency as that they bare down the Guards, and put a whole Regiment of Horse in disorder, whereby the whole Army taking the Alarum, the *English* charged them so home as that they put them into a rout, and pursued them within half a League of *Edinbourgh*, killing them a sufficient number both of Officers and Souldiers, and taking several prisoners: After which, the Scots being disgusted at these their ill successes, retired themselves for a while within their intrenchments, where we shall also leave them to their closer guards. In the meanwhile the Parliament interdicted the Commerce between *England* and *Scotland*, and caused their Ships to be adjudged good Prize, which contributed very much to their undoing and ruine: During which they wanted for no Partisanes in *England*, who laboured to dispose things toward the effecting of their grand design, and amongst their chief Agitators, Collonel *Eusebius Andrewes* being discovered and convinced, was also condemned and beheaded on *Tower-hill*.

The whole Moneth of *August* passed almost away without any action in *Scotland*, towards the latter end whereof, *Collington* and *Readhall* were taken by attempt, where the Lord *Hamilton* and Major *Hamilton* were taken, with 60. Souldiers, 60. Barrels of Powder, Armes for 60 men, and a considerable quantity of Victuals, and other good Booty, all which hapned on the 24 of *August*.

E   After

After which the whole Body of the English Army quitted the Mountains of *Pentland*, and encamped about *Collington* and *Readhall*, and the parts adjacent within one Mile of the Scotch Army; on the seven and twentieth both Armies marched Flank to Flank, being only seperated by a little Quagmire or Marsh-ground, which hindred their Conjunction, however the Canon played upon each other, and on the 28th the English Canon plyed the Scots hard, and endamaged them very much, notwithstanding they neither quitted their Ground, nor would they come to a Resolution to joyn in a closer Fight. And the English having consumed all their Provisions of Victualls, retired unto their former Quarters, first unto *Pentland* Hills, and afterwards unto *Musselborough* whither they had much ado to reach, where being somewhat refreshed, they dreyned their Garisons, assembled also their Forces, and took their March toward *Haddington*, at which the Scots coasting their March on their right Wing, did charge them with a Squadron of stout Men, and as they did most briskly set upon the English, so they were in like manner vigorously repulst by a Regiment of Foot commanded by Colonel *Fairfax*: On the first day of *September* both Armies found themselves only seperated by the Town and the Scots, being encamped in an advantagious place, on the West-side of the Town the English were engaged to encamp themselves on the East-side of the Town, in an open Field, very

very fit to give Battel in, without that either
Party would give or take advantage of the
Ground, where the English having attended the
Enemies a sufficient space of time, and perceiving that they would not fight but upon an advantage,they took their March towards *Dunbar*,
whither the Scots followed them immediatly,
and at a certain passage endeavoured to charge
their Rearguard; But the English immediatly
facing about, the Scots changed their resolution
and gained the Hills, where they thought they
might with advantage cut off the English their
passage oo *Coperspeth* : at which time the English
Army was but in a very ill Condition, the
Winter wᶜʰ begins betimes in those parts had so
nipt them with Colds and great Rains, and the
ill Victuals which theyhad besides, caused a great
deal of sickness in the Army, Fluxes, Loosness,
and other Diseases, whereby many died, and
were rendred uncapable of Service, being sent
and carried away to *Barwick*, and the adjoyning
parts.

The Scots who very well knew the sad estate
of the English Army, which they had really
blocked up at the passage of *Copperspeth*, which
is betwixt *Dunbar* and *Barwick*, thereby impe-
ding the English's Communication with that
place, and by hindring them from those Conveniencies which they thence received, intending
either to overcome them there, or to cause them
to perish there for want of Necessaries, so that
they promised themselves an unquestionable

Victory

Victory without much loss on their sides, wherby they presumed to brag that they had gotten the English in the Earl of *Essex*'s Penfold, alluding to that extremity whereunto the Royallists had reduced that Earle in the County of *Cornwall*, where his Army surrendred at discretion (the Horse only excepted, who made their way through the Enemy in the Night-time.) Nor were the Scots their hopes ill grounded, considering the ill plight wherein the English Army was at that time, and the inequality of their Forces, the Scots being at the least 20000 Men, and the English not above 12000, divers of which were likewise sick: But the extremity whereunto the English were reduced, made them pitch upon so firm a resolution, either to overcome, or to die in the Battel; as that the Scots were totally routed and defeated, by those very reasons, and that very confidence which had made them as it were sure of the Victory. Wherefore the General, and the chief Officers of the English Army, deeming that the longer they should delay, to put it to a noble adventure, whereby to get out of this great straight wherein they were, the lesse they should be able to [compass it, resolved either to make their passage through their Enemies by the points of their Swords, or to perish in the undertaking; So that they imployed the whole Night in seeking of the Lord, and imploring his Assistance from Heaven, as also in giving out and distributing the Orders requisite for the Fight,

The Battel of *Dunbar* gained by the *English*

and

and just at break of the day, the Army was ready drawn up into Battel-aray, and to give the on-set; the English word was, *The Lord of Hoastes*: and the Scots word was, *The Covenant*, which did very well represent the state of their Affairs, and the subject of their Quarrell, and in an instant both the English Horse and Foot, with a gallant resolution, fiercely charged the right Wing of the Scots; where the Enemy had placed all their *Cavalry*, on purpose to hinder the English in their passage that way. The Scots received their Charge with a great deal of constancy and resolution, and it may justly be said, That *Alexander* did not meet with more resistance, nor glory at the passage of *Granicia*, then our late Protector met with at this Encounter; especially if so be we consider, how that the said Conquerour of *Asia* had to do with an effeminate kind of People, bred in a delicious Country, accustomed to their ease and pleasures; but here on the contrary, That the English brought up in a fertile abundant Soil, and under a middle Climate, should come to confront a War-like Nation in a harsh, barren, and cold Climat. The General's own Regiment of Foot had the Vanguard that day, and performed the parts of men, answering most gloriously to that honour which belonged to them: Their Colonel and General together animating and encouraging them by his own example; witnessed by his Actions, that there was not a straws breadth that day betwixt them and death

or

or the Victory: Major General *whaley* charged the Enemies whole Army through and through, with his Regiment; bearing down all those who durst withstand him, and without the loss of many men; having wheeled about again, and cleared all before him, regained his former station himself, having only received a flight Wound in the Arm, and had a Horse killed under him. And not to detain the Reader in any further suspence, all the Regiments of the Army performing their parts, like resolute gallant men, (For should a man go about to praise one Squadron or Battallion of them in particular, he must of necessity derogate from the rest) you might have observed as many Soldiers as Officers, & as many Officers as Soldiers, who being all of them animated, or rather inspired by a supernaturall instinct of Valour, a man would have thought they had been invulnerable, or shot-free, and that a Hand from on high did defend them from the showers of Lead and Launces, which were ready to overwhelme them, so that the violence and force wherewith they fought, did only permit the Scots to put by their Blows, as also it is worthy to be noted that in all this Fight the English lost but forty men, whereas of the Scots there were foure thousand killed upon the place, and that Army which was stronger then the English by two thirds, thinking to have overwhelmed them, did only by closing in upon them, force them to fight with the greater vigour; and you would
have

have imagined, that the little Army of the English consisted only of one Body, which had but one only motion, and charged the Enemy on all sides with so much Impetuosity and Animosity, as that you would have said it had been and insensible Mass, or Lump which only pressed forwards, where the weight of Arms, or the force of Powder did transport it. Finally, after one whole hours dispute, very hot Fight, and violent furious Contests, the Scots gave way, and their Horse being put to flight, endeavoured to save themselves by the goodness of their heels, the English Cavalry pursuing them to *Haddington*, all the Scotch Foot remained on the place, and that which rendred the slaughter of them the greater was, that the English Soldiers remembred an Action which hapned the day before, in which thirty Soldiers of Colonel *Prides* Regiment being commanded to possess a House scituate betwixt both Camps, and not being seconded, were over-powred by a greater number of the Scots , and so forced to deliver up the place again, notwithstanding which, after they had promised quarter to the English, they killed three of them, and hurt all the rest : There was no English Soldiers but had a Prisoner in this Battel, there being taken ten thousand, most of all which, except the Officers, were suffered to steal away, amidst which there was ten Colonels, twelve Lievetenant Colonels, nine Majors, forty seven Captains, seventy two Lievetenants, and eighty Ensigns, and amongst the Pri-

E 4   soners

soners of Quality, there was the Lord *Libberton*,
and his Son, the Lord *Chrifton*, Sir *James Lundf-*
dale, Livetenant Generall of the Foot, and Sir
Phlierth Adjutant General, all their Baggage
and Canon was taken, to the number of two
and twenty great Guns, and leverall leffer ones,
two hundred Colours; and Armes for 15000
Men, of the Englifh there was but one Officer
killed, and Major *Rook by*, who afterwards died
of his Wounds; as also Captain *Sloyd* of
the Lord *Fleetwoods* Regiment, dangeroufly
wounded. His late Highness obtained this memorable Victory on the third day of *September*,
1650, on which day he also obtained another
no lefs famous then this: And on this very day
God crowned his Labours with a peacefull and
refolved quiet death, whereby he no less triumphed over the World, and the rage of Hell,
then he did in this laft Battel we have related,
over a most puiffant raging Enemy; at which
time his Army, as a man may fay (brought low
by Want, and Sicknelles) was even Bedrid,
and at deaths very Door. And as the Parliament of *England* had caufed a day of univerfall
Prayers and Faftings to be kept for the good
fuccefs of their Army in *Scotland*; To likewife
did they order a day of generall Thanfgiving for
this fo notable and famous Victory: and the
Generall likewife on his part did not faile with
the whole Army, to acknowledge the good
Handy work of God, who had fo vifibly gained
him and them this Battel: And the better to

prosecute

prosecute the said Victory, and to reap the fruits thereof, On the seventh day of *September,* four Regiments of Foot were sent to possess *Lieth,* a very considerable and advantageous place, where seven and thirty piece of Ordnance were found mounted on Plat-forms, and a considerable quantity both of Ammunitions of War and Provisions of Victuals. And on the same day his late Highness became Master of the City of *Edinbrough,* the Metropolitan of all *Scotland,* and caused his whole Army to march into it, without any loss, save the Arme of one Soldier, which was shot off by a Canon-bullet from the Castle. And on the next Lords-day he sent a Trumpeter to the Castle, to give notice to such Ministers as had abandoned their Pulpits, to come and perform their Duties in their said Callings, which they having refused to do, he caused English Ministers to Officiate in their places; in the mean while, all possible diligence was used in the Fortifying of *Lieth,* it being concluded to be the best and most commodious sheltring-place the English could have in *Scotland,* for the Winter Season. And after his late Highness had by sound of Trumpet, both at *Lieth* and *Edinbrough,* caused the freedome of Traffick, and liberty of Trade to be published and established, a sure way for the publick Markets, himself on the fourteenth marched toward *Nethrife,* six miles from *Edinbrough,* leaving Major General *Overton* with his Brigade in *Edinborough.* On the fifteenth the Army advanced

Lieth taken.

Edinbrough taken.

advanced toward *Linlithgo*, but by reason of the ill Weather they could not pass on forward; On the sixteenth, they marched toward *Falkirk*, and the next day they came up within one mile of *Sterling*; On the eighteenth, the Councel of War being assembled, a Letter was drawn up to be sent thither, by which the tendemess and affection of the English towards the Scotch Nation was represented, alledging that though formerly it had not taken its defired effects; Notwithstanding, feeing that at prefent the Fortune and Succefs of Armes had been fo contrary to them, they defired them to reflect on thofe Propofals which had been formerly made unto them, and to furrender that place unto them, for the ufe of the Common-wealth of *England*, and a Trumpeter being fent with the aforefaid Letter, who coming up almoft to the VValls, met with a Gentleman on foot, with a Pike in his hand, who told him he fhould not be fuffered to come into the place, and that his Letter fhould in like manner not be received: In the Afternoon that very day, thofe of the Town fent a Trumpeter, to demand the Prifoners, with a proffer to pay their Ranfoms; To whom the General made anfwer, *That they were not come into* Scotland *to trade in Men, nor to enrich themfelves, but to do Service to the Common-wealth of* England, *and to fettle and eftablifh thofe Dominions.* On the fame day, Orders were iffued to draw up the whole Army to the very VValls of the Town, and by fetting fcaling

Ladders

Ladders to the place, to give a generall Assault, but after it was found that there was but a little appearance to effect the same, in regard of the good Condition the Place and Garison was in, they changed their resolution, and on the nineteenth the Army retired to *Linlithgow*, which was accounted a very fit place to make a Garison of, whereby both *Sterling* and *Edinborough* might be bridled and curbed, and the necessary Orders for the fortifying of the place being given, there were five Troops of Horse left in Garison, and six Companies of Foot, and the Body of the Army returned to *Edinborough*, where on the twenty third of *September*, there was a day of Humiliation celebrated and solemnly kept.

And much about the same time the Churches of *Scotland* likewise ordered a solemn Festivall for the ensuing Reasons ; *Viz.*

I. *To humble themselves before God, and to crave his pardon for having too much relyed on the Arme of Flesh.*

II. *For the wickedness and profaneness of their Armies.*

III. *For the Spoils and other Misdemeanours their Soldiers had committed in England.*

IV. *For*

IV. *For having not sufficiently purged their Armies; that is to say, For not having put out such persons as were not godly, and of their Belief.*

V. *For the indirect and sinister Means which their Commissioners made use of in their Treaty with their King, and the indirect wayes by which they had brought him into* Scotland.

VI. *For their not having sufficiently purged the Kings Family.*

VII. *For the just Grounds they had to believe that his Majesties repentance was not really and from his heart.*

The besieging of *Edinborough* Ca-   The rest of the Month was imployed in the making of the Siege and Approaches against the Castle of *Edinborough*, and in applying the Mines to the Walls. And on the thirtieth the English with so much gallantry surprized one of their Bulwarks, as they carried thence three hundred Muskets, one Ensign, and severall other Armes, without the loss of one Man. On the first of *October*, the Besieged began to make their

Salleys

Salleys to hinder the working of the Miners, upon whom they fired inceſſantly with their great and ſmall Shot, yet however they continued their Sappinges. Upon the ſecond of the ſaid Month, upon notice that ſeverall Armes and Ammunitions of VVar were hidden in the Cathedrall Church at *Edinborough* they were tranſported thence. VVhilſt the fortifying of *Leith* was carried on vigorouſly, as well as the Mines under the Caſtle of *Edinborough*, that no time might be loſt; his late Highneſs whoſe great Soul could not live without Action, and who was not to be taken up by one or two ſingle Objects, marched off with part of the Army to go and view *Glaſcow*, which having done, and finding that he was not in a Condition to aſſail it at that time, he returned back to *Edinborough*; but by the way, he raſed two ſtrong Holds whither the *Moſs Troopers* were accuſtomed to retreat and ſhelter. And as the *Scots* had a puiſſent Enemy in the heart of their Country, ſo had they a far greater in their very Bowels, ſince its generally confeſt, That the greateſt of all Evils which can poſſibly happen to a State, Is the Diviſions which the different profeſſions in Religion, and the other particular Intereſts do beget: For in the North of *Scotland*, there was a Party for the King, ſeperated from the Churches, in the VVeſt, there was a Party for the Church ſeperated from the King; ſo likewiſe there was a third Party more moderate, who held both for King and Church, and all theſe inteſtine

stine Divisions were carryed on with such a violent animosity, as that they neglected the common good, and were even ready to eat each others throat: The last of these parties was the strongest, being composed of the General States of the Kingdome, as then held at *Sterling*, who neverthelesse stood upon their Guards, as well as the several others did, they being afraid of each other. The Assembly of the Estates used their best endeavours to reconcile these two parties, and to this purpose treated mainly with the Colonels *Carre* and *Straughan*, who seemed to be the chief Heads of the said parties; but they could not prevail with them. His late Highnesse who was alwayes as politick as vigilant, endeavoured to make good use of their dissentions, and so wrote both unto *Carre* and *Straughan*, but their particular quarrels hindred them not to joyn in their general animosities against the *English*, whom they reputed to be their common Enemy. But the said proffers which were made unto them, having as little wrought upon them as the care of their own preservations, Colonel *Whaley* was commanded with a good Squadron of the Army, to goe and reduce them to their obedience, which he undertook not, however, before he had once more assayled to gain them by fair means, wherefore he sent a Letter unto them both, representing unto them in substance as followeth, *viz.*

Tha

That all the world knew how many amicable wayes and endeavours had been used by the *English* since their being in *Scotland*, to hinder the effusion of Christian blood; and although all the said undertakings had proved fruitlesse, yet they still harboured the same thoughts and resolutions, continuing thus, that their arms were alwayes ready and open to receive and embrace them, whensoever it should please God to inspire them to meet them half-way. That their design was not to rule over them, nor to intrench upon their liberties, far lesse on their Church Government, or to possesse their goods and fortunes, their drift being only to advance the Lords work: But if they perished in their blindnesse, and would continue to harbour frivolous and vain hopes, they must continue to be their enemies to their rests, and declared unto them, that all the miseries which should befall them hereafter, either by the sword or famine, would fall very heavy on their own accompt.

Collonel Carr sent an answer to this Letter quite in another strain then it might have been expected from persons who professed to desire nothing so much as an accommodation; and this Answer was returned to Commissary General *Whaley*, in his being at *Carlisle*, according to the tenour following, or very nigh the same: That although they were not strong enough to resist the *English* their unjust Invasion, yet that they had strength enough to undergoe

dergoe it, and that by their actions and sufferings they would submit themselves to the will of God, untill the time of their deliverance should come : That in case they should have the happinesse to perish in doing of their duties, it would be too much grace that God would do unto them, that they doubted not but, when their miseries should be arrived at the full pitch, their Fortune would then change, adding that they thought it very strange, that the *English* should mention a cessation of Arms at the same time when they laded their Subjects with Irons, when they took their Townes, when they imprisoned their Ministers, and by this means bereaved their flocks (now going astray) of the only and best comforts which they had left unto them amidst their greatest miseries : Concluding thus, That if they would voluntarily desert and relinquish *Scotland,* and afterwards enter upon a Treaty in such a manner as becommeth Christians to doe, it would be a reciprocal grace and favour they would doe unto both Nations. But these Interparlies having proved thus unprofitable, the *English* began to fall to work again, and Major *Brown* possessed himself of a strong place called *Bull-house,* and afterwards took the Castle of *Dorlington,* in which there were great store of Ammunitions of warre found, and in this last some Mosse-Troopers, some of which were put to death. Collonel *Monke* likewise with a party, both of Horse and Foot, marched towards the Castle

of

of *Rozellar* within seven miles of *Edinborough,* which was also surrendred after some Granado Shells were fired into it : Immediately after which Colonel *Lambert* marched with 2000 Horse towards *Dumfreez,* in quest of Colonel *Carre* who was about *Peblies,* and likewise Colonel *Whalley* who commanded a Squadron of that partie, took *Dalkeith* on his march, which meerly surrendred upon the threats which he sent in unto those who defended it, although the walls of the said Castle were 13 foot thick, and that they were well stored with Canon, Arms, and all kinde of warlike Ammunitions, and provisions of victuals. Mean-while Colonel *Lambert* having with much difficulty passed the River *Hamilton,* encamped there that night, whereof Colonel *Carre* having notice, did endeavour to surprize him the next morning at the very break of day, which he likewise did very briskly, but the *English* having opportunely taken the Alarum, and being unwilling that any of the Enemies forces should escape out of their hands, did surround them in such a manner, as that they found themselves at one and the self same time set upon on all sides. The *English* in a trice killed them 100 men, and took as many pri-soners: Nor could the Scotch Horse escape their clutches, so that they dismounted 400 Horse-men, whose Horses and baggage they brought away, and might have had the men too, but that they would not stand to trouble themselves with so many Prisoners, but rather

F   follow

follow the Run-awayes, and so contented themselves to take the most confiderable persons:
They chased the Scots as farre as *Air* Town:
Colonel *Kerre* himself was wounded and taken Prisoner, together with his Captain-Lieu-
tenant, as well as his Lievtenant-Colonel and
Major *Straughon*: as for Captain *Giffin*, and
several other chief Officers of their partcys
they came and voluntarily surrendred themselves up to Major Generall *Lambert*; who
brought them all with him to the Head quarters at *Edinborough*. During all which, the
approaches against *Edinborough* Castle, were
continued, but to speak the truth, with little
or no effect, till the Moneth of *December*;
when as all the Troops which were disperfed
up and down the Countrey, were assembled
and brought together, by reason of the ill weather and sharp season, which would not permit them any longer to keep the field, and
then they fell to work in earnest towards the
reducing of the said Castle, which is the strong-
eft and most confiderable of all that Countrey,
against which a Plat-form was raised to place
the Morter-pieces and the great Guns on, but
those within relyed so much on the strength
and goodnesse of the place, that they hung out
a Flagge of defiance; but not long after they
were glad to take it in again, whereby it was
conceived that the Morter-shells had done
some execution, and that thereby they were
constrained to change their title; so that in

tein

lieu of their former Flagge, they were glad to hang out a white one, betokening Peace, and likewise they sent out a Drummer to propound, That they were resolved to yield, if so be they might be permitted to send to the Deputy of the States, which being refused them, they desired to parley, and so delivered up the place. Moreover one of the most remarkable and essential parts of his Highnesse life, was his ability in making choice of capable personages, fit to serve the State as well by their Councels, as for the managing of the wars, and indeed herein the Parliament alwayes preferred his opinion and sence beyond all others, having found by experience, that his advice and counsells were accompanyed with a good fortune, as his valour constrayned her to Crown his actions.

And on the other part, Generall *Blake*, who commanded the Common-wealths Fleet at Sea, was no lesse successefull by Sea then his late Highnesse was by Land, whose Naval Forces being anchored before *Lisbone*, having taken severall *French* and *Portugal* men of war, which much endamaged the *English* Merchant-men, especially those which traded to the *Levant*, was obliged by ill weather and for want of provisions, to quit that Coast, and to leave the Port of *Lisbone* free.

The good successe of the Naval Forces under Generall Blake.

During which, Prince *Rupert* making use of this opportunity, set sail towards *Mallaga*, where he took, burnt, and pillaged severall *English* Merchant-men, which obliged Admirall

Blake to reduce his Fleet to seven of his best
sailing Frigats, and sending the rest into *England*
with the Prizes which he had taken, he pursued
the Enemies with all possible speed & diligence,
and being arrived at *Mallaga,* he understood
that they had made sail towards *Alicant,* and
in his search of them, betwixt the Cape of
Gat and *Paulo,* he took a *French* Ship, which
carryed twenty Guns, and presently afterwards
the *Roe-buck* of Prince *Ruperts* Fleet, after
which he encountred with another called the
Black Prince, which rather then she would suffer
her self to be taken, ran on shore, and fired her
powder: Some few dayes after four Vessels
more of Prince *Ruperts* Fleet ran on shoare in
the Bay of *Carthagena,* where they were lost,
and deserted by their Ships Companies: Infomuch that of all that Fleet, there was but two
left, which steered their course toward *Major-
ca* and *Sumaterra.*   Generall *Blake* having thus
missed them, would no longer continue the
pursuit, lest the Common-wealth might need
him on more urgent and important occasions,
so that he set over for *England,* to receive the
Laurels due to his good service, having done
as much as could be expected from a person of
Honour and Courage, alwayes faithfull and
true to the Common-wealth. He was received
by the Parliament with all the prayse and
thanks he could expect for his good service, but
especially by the Merchants, who treated him
highly, and immediately revived the Trade
                                        again

Prince
Ruperts
Fleet rui-
ned.

again, which had for so long time as it were
layn dead by the interruptions of so many Enemies. Notwithstanding which good successes
the Royallists were not backwark to be stirring
in *England*, being incited thereunto by the Ministers of the old Church of *England*, one of
their Agents *Benson* being discovered, was put
to death: So likewise in the County of *Norfolk* certain people made a rising, and under the
notion of abolishing Papisme, Schismes and
Heresies, and of re-establishing the King, they
gathered to a head, but the Parliament not giving them time to get into a body, they were
routed and defeated, and a score of them were
put to death. Much about which time there
happened a contest at *Constantinople* betwixt
two *English* Ambassadors, the one a Royallist,
the other a Common-wealths-man, and to
know which was the true Ambassador, they
referred their businesse to the
who delivered the Royallist into the others
power, to dispose of him as he pleased, and in
reference thereto he was imbarqued at *Smyrna*
for *London*, where he was beheaded before the
Exchange.

But to return to *Scotland*, where the cold
Northern Climate seems to have buryed all the
Martial heat, although not the *Scotch* Ministers
zeal, who had excommunicated *Straughon* and
Swinton, for adhering to the *English*, who performed in those parts as much as the rigour of
the season would permit men to doe, and the

Scots on the other side laboured to unite and settle each others mindes and differences, give order for new Levies, and Crowned their King with the greatest magnificence as the indigency and necessity of their affairs would permit. The *Scots*, who were better accustomed to the rigour and violence of their Winters then the *English*, thinking to have some advantage over them, would not let slip so favourable a season without their making some good use thereof, wherefore Lievtenant General *David Lesly*, With a party of 800 Horse endeavoured to surprize *Lithgoe*, maintained but by one Regiment of Horse, under the Command of Colonel *Sanderson*, but finding the *English* upon their guards, were forced to return without any attempt at all : And the *English* on the other side, to let them see that the harsh season had not quite benummed them, took the field with two Regiments, one of Horse, the other of Foot, commanded by Colonel *Fenwick*, and marched towards the taking of *Hume* Castle, which was very strong by reason of its situation ; I have here inserted two Letters which passed between the Besiegers and the Besieged, by reason that the one denotes an absolute power in the Countrey, and the other bears an extraordinary style.

TO

TO THE

GOVERNOUR

OF the CASTLE of

H U M E.

SIR,

HIs Excellency the Lord General Crom-well, Hath commanded me to reduce to his Obedience the Castle which you keep; In case you deliver it into my Hands for his Service, it shall be on such Articles which may please you, and those which are with you, by which means you will not a little ease the Neighbouring Countries about you: In case you give me a refusall, I doubt not but by Gods assistance to obtain that which at present I demand of you; I expect your Answer to Morrow by seven in the Morning, and remain your Servant

FENVVICK.

THE
ANSVVER:
To the GOVERNOUR of
BARWICK,
Colonel *FENWICK.*

Right Honrable,

I Have seen a Trumpet of yours, as he saith, without a Pass, who doth summon me to surrender the Castle of *Hume* to the Lord General *Cromwell*; That it may not displease you, I never did see nor know your General: as for the Castle of *Hume,* it is seated on a Rock. Given in the Castle of *Hume* this day, before seven of the Clock. In these terms I do remain, without prejudice to my Country, your most humble Servant

Tho. Cockburne.

But

BUt the Morter-pieces had no sooner made a slight breach, when as they demanded to parley, and because they would not receive such Conditions as were preferred unto them, they were forced to be contented with such Conditions as they could obtain, and thus they surrendred at discretion. After which, Colonel *Monke* with about three Regiments of Horse and Foot laid siege to *Tymptallon* Castle, which for the space of eight and forty hours together, he battered with Morter-pieces without any effect, whereby he was enforced to raise a Battery of six Guns, which did marvellous execution, whereupon the besieged desired to parley, but no composition would be given them, so that at last they were constrained to yield to the mercy of the Conquerour, and to deliver into his hand all the Armes, Cannon, Ammunitions of War, and Provisions ; The keeping of which Place by the *Scots*, was a shrewd Thorn in the sides of the *English*, who were by the parties from the said Castle scituate between *Edinborough* and *Barwick* daily taken and dispoiled, when as they stragled never so little out of their way, which enforced his late Highness to cause this ensuing Declaration to be published, and to have executed with the utmost rigour ; *Viz.*

A Decla-

A

DECLARATION

By GENERAL

CROMWEL.

A Decla-
ration for
the securi-
ty of the
Soldiers.

Finding that severall who bear Armes under our Colours, are stript, robbed, and most barbarously and inhumanely murthered by Thieves and Vagabonds, who are not under discipline of any Army; And moreover that the Inhabitants of these Parts, instead of answering our goodness, do joyne with such people and support them; And considering that it is in the power of the said Inhabitants, to discover and produce them, since they do for the

most

most part dwell round about those places, where usually the said Villanies are committed ; Observing moreover, that by the Intelligence which is given by the Peasants, the said Robbers come forth of their lurking places. Therefore I do declare, That in whatsoever place it shal happen, that any of our Men shall be robbed and dispoiled, or killed by such like persons ; I shall require life for life, and an entire restitution for those things which shall be so stoln, upon the Villages, and other places, where the Fact shall have been committed, unless they discover and produce the Malefactor : And hereof I will that all men take knowledge, that none may pretend cause of Ignorance herein. Given under my Hand and Seal at *Edinborough* 5. *November* 1656.

Signed, *O. Cromwell.*

BY vertue of this Proclamation severall summs of money were raised on those Parishes and places where the like Robberies and Murthers were committed, and those who were found either to be the Authors of, or Complices therein, in any manner whatsoever, were either put to death, or put to a pecuniary Mulct. Shortly after there was a design upon *Brunt* Island, but at that time it took not any effect; whereas General *Cromwell* drew all his Forces out of *Edinborough*, to have maintained them all the rest of the Winter in *Fyfe*, which is the best part of all *Scotland*, but the rigour of the Season, and the difficulty of the passage constrained him to face about again to his old Quarters, which were very good by reason of the Shipping which continually arived at *Leith* with all kind of Provisions for the Soldiery Horse and Foot; which said Refreshments came in very good time to the Army, which being not accustomed to the extream rigour of the Weather in those Parts, was incommodated by severall Diseases, and amongst the rest, by a certain contagious Feaver which is peculiar to that Country, and the which had also seised the General himself, who spared his person no more then the least Soldier; His late Highness was so cast down by this kind of Contagion, as that it was believed he would scarce have escaped death; and it may be said that his sickness was the greatest of the whole Armies, for the private Soldiers they

lost

loft no Courage, but did gladly and joyfully withstand and out-brave those difficulties which stopped *Julius Cæsar* in his enterprize in those parts, and who chose rather to bear the charge of a prodigious VVall which fenced him from the Scotch Incursions, then to engage his Army in that mountainous Country, hoary with Snow and Ice, and the Conquest whereof was by the English undertaken in the very heart of the VVinter.

And whilst the fierceness of the VVinter is passing over, we will leave both parties in *Scotland*, being seperated by a River, which was impossible to be passed over in that Season, and will make a small digression into *England*, to see what in the mean while passed there. At *Oxford*, one of the most famous Universities of *England*, A certain Maiden, who by mischance at four Months end cast her Fruit, was accused, to have done it wilfully and of set purpose, to have used some art therein; and without any more formalities) was Impeached and condemned to be hanged, which was accordingly done; and some while afterwards the Physicians and Chirurgions being resolved to make a dissection of her body; there being no Symptomes of life at all in her: Notwithstanding, just as they were ready to cut her up, as if she had been only in a Dream, and as if her shamefac'dness, being not able to endure the touching and looks of so many men, had awakened her, to shut their Eyes and Rasors, she gave some tokens of

of life, to the admiration of the wisest and most
judicious men learned in the like Cases, who
all of them declared, that she was really dead;
whereupon no kind of remedies were left unaf-
failed to bring her to herself, which accordingly
was accomplished, and she at present liveth
in as perfect health as ever she did before; It
being not Gods will nor pleasure, that during
the Government of the justest of Conquerours,
there should an act of so high an Injustice pass,
as the barbarous condemning and putting to
death so innocent a Creature, as the Event proved this silly Maiden to be.

But to come to publick Concernments, the
Parliament being desirous together with the
Kings person to extirpate his Memory, and to
remove those Objects which might beget tenderness in the people, (who do alwaies bemoan
the misfortunes of those whom before they ha-
ted) Commanded that his Statues should be
flung down, whereupon that which stood on
the West-end of St. *Pauls* Church in *London*
was cast down, and the other which was placed
in the old *Exchange*, placing this following In-
scription in the Compartment above the same;
*Exit tyrannus Regum ultimus Anno Libertatis
Angliae restitutae primo, Anno Domini, 1648. Janu-
arii* 30. In like manner the Armes of the Crown
of *England*, which were placed in the Churches,
in the Courts of Judicature, and other publick
places, were taken down. And the Common-
weath being now as it seemed solidly established,

ed, some neighbouring States who desired to be in Amity with Her, sent their extraordinary Ambassadors over; as namely, the *Hollanders*, *Spain* and *Portugals* and by the following Negociations the issues of the said Embassies will easily appear.

As to the *Spanish* Ambassador, satisfaction was continually demanded of him, for the Murther which was committed on the persons of this Common-wealths Agents at *Madrid*, nor was this State at all satisfied with the Answer thereon returned; That the Contestations between the King of *Spain* and his Clergy, on that particular were not as yet reconciled or brought to a issue. And as to the *Portugal* Ambassador, great and vast summes being demanded of him for the reimbursement of those Charges which the King his Master had caused the Common-wealth to be at, and for the reparation of those damages which the English Merchants had sustained: He replyed, he had no Orders to make Answer thereunto; whereupon he had his Audience of departure, and went his way.

Immediatly after, this Common-wealth sent two extraordinary Ambassadors to the States of the united Provinces, the Lords *Oliver St. Johns*, and *Walter Strickland*, Personages of a high repute, and endowed with exquisite Parts; their Train was great ad splendid, and their Equipage savoured not a little of the Splendor of their continued Victories: They Embarqued in the *Downs* on the eleventh of *March*, 1651. and the

next

next day toward even they came to an anchor neer *Helvoet Slugs,* but not without some danger, on the 13 they made towards *Rotterdam* in the long-boats, and by the way they were met by some of the States Jachts or Barges, and being arrived they were by the *English* Merchants conducted to their publick House, where they were most splendidly entertained; whither the *Spanish* Ambassador sent to complement them, by one of his Gentlemen, to testifie unto them his joy for their happy arrival, beseeching them to enter into and joyn with him in a right understanding. Two or three dayes after, they set forward towards the *Hague,* and by the way were met by the Master of Ceremonies, accompanyed with about thirty Coaches, and after some reciprocal complements passed and exchanged, they were conducted to a stately House which was prepared for them in the Town, where having been three dayes treated at the States charges, they had audience. In which the Lord St. *Johns* made a most Elegant and learned Speech, in *English,* and gave the Copy thereof unto the Lords States both in *English* and in *Dutch,* the most essential points whereof were as followeth.

I. *That*

I. *That they were sent unto the Lords, the High and mighty States of the United Provinces, on the behalf of the Parliament of the Common-wealth of* England, *to cement a firm League and Confederation betwixt the two Common-wealths, in case their Lordships thought it fitting, notwithstanding the injuries which the* English *had received from the* Holland *Nation.*

II. *That they desired to renew and confirm the Treaties and Agreements formerly made, concerning the Traffique and Commerce betwixt both Nations.*

III. *After which they exhibited the advantages which the* Hollanders *would reap by this said union, in regard of the commodious situation of* England, *for the Traffique, with the multitude and security of her Havens, and of all things which may advance the Commerce and Trade.*

IV. *Finally he told them, That he was commanded by the Parliament of* England *and by the Common-wealth, to make known* to their Lordships, how sencibly they were touched with the Murder which was committed on the person of their Agent, Mr. Dorislaus, and that they doubted not but their Lordships would use all possible endeavours to discover the Authors of that horrid and unworthy action.

After which, the Lords States being informed, that the said Lords Ambassadors followers were daily molested and affronted by the *English* Royallists, and other persons, who resided in *Holland*, they caused a Proclamation to be drawn up, which they sent up to the Lords Ambassadors, to know of them whether it was penned in the due terms, according to their good liking, whereby on pain of death they prohibited, that no man should either by words or deeds, offend or molest any of the said Ambassadors followers or retainers. Three months time was already elapsed in their Negotiation at a vast expense, and with a farre greater patience, without that the least satisfaction in the world could be obtained at the hands of Justice, for those daily affronts & injuries which were put upon the Lords Ambassadors Retinue & Servants, and the scorns and disgraces offered to their own persons, even to such a pitch, as that the Common people and Rascality would assemble themselves at the Gates of their house, and belch out injurious language, and set upon, and injure

injure their Servants. Now the Parliament being sensible of these wrongs and injuries, and seeing the Lords States did not at all answer those kinde proffers and endeavours which were made unto them, to beget and settle a solid and firm alliance and peace betwixt the two Common-wealths, save with delayes and shifts, purposely to gain time upon the *English*, till they should be able to judge how the face of things would evidence it self in *Scotland*, and which way the Chain would turn there, they recalled their Ambassadors.

Which suddain and unexpected newes extreamly surprised the *Hollanders*, who testified their astonishments thereon to the Lords Ambassadors, by more frequent and oftner visitations then formerly, and by which they endeavoured to perswade them to beleeve the sincerity of their intentions, and how earnestly and ardently they desired the alliance which their Lordships had propounded. But all these fair words were not able to stay the Ambassadors, who immediately returned into *England* again, to cut out another guesse kinde of work for the *Hollanders*. And that which gave the greater cause of jealousie unto the *English*, and made them believe that the *Hollander* dealt deceitfully with them, was that their Admirall *Van Trump* lay lurking about the Isle of of *Scillie*, with his Fleet, as if he had some design to make himself Master of them: But when as the States were demanded the reason of his

lying

lying there, they replyed, that their Admirals being in those parts was only to demand restitution of some Ships, Goods and Merchandises which the Pyrats of those parts had despoiled their Merchants of: Which answer though in some measure it satisfied the Parliament, yet not so farre as to trust too much therein to the *Hollanders,* and whereby the Parliament was obliged to give order for the suddain reducing of that Island to their obedience.

The reducing the Isle of *Scilly.*

Generall *Blake* being re-inforced by a Squadron of Ships commanded by Sir *George Askue* which was designed for the reduceing of the *Cariba* Islands made sail towards *Scilly,* where immediately they set ashoar 300. Sea-men, besides the Land-men, the Sea-men gave the first onset with a great deal of courage and resolution, and the Land-men did second them very well, insomuch that they speedily became Masters of the Isles of *Tresco* and *Bryers,* where they took 150 Prisoners, after they had once slain a score of them. They found in the place two good Frigats, one of 18 Guns and the other of 32. and immediately possessed the best Haven of all these Islands, whence the Enemies fled unto *St. Maries,* the strongest of all those Islands, but which held not long out afterwards, and so they were all reduced. It is unnecessary to lose time in the dilating upon the strength and conveniencies of those Islands, since all what art and nature could possibly allotte unto them, is there to be found, and so

need

need but look into the Mappes, to judge by their very situation, of what concernment they are unto *England*. Meanwhile it is worthy admiration that so difficult a Conquest should be attained in so little a space of time, with the losse of so few men onely. And whereas the Royallists did continue to make good *Cornet* Castle in the Isle of *Guernsey*, and on a false advise, that there were but forty men in the place, eighteen of which were also said to be incapable of doing service, a resolution was taken to set upon the said Castle, and to carry it by surprisall; but when the attempt was made, there were found to be in the place threescore good men, who when the Scaleing Ladders were applyed to the walls, and the assault given to the place, defended themselves resolutely, and endammaged the Assailants in such a manner, with Stones and Timber which they cast down upon them, as also by their Canon which flanked the wall, charged with Case-shot, as that they killed divers of the Assailants, and constrayned the rest to retire, and the greatest dysaster that hapned, was, that a Vessel or two in which the men retired, were sunk by the Canon from the Castle. And however this attempt did not succeed, yet the *English* did like couragious men, and deserved no lesse prayse then if they had carryed the place. About which time, one *Brown-Bushell* was beheaded at *London*, a famous Royallist both by Sea and Land, for having deserted the Parliaments Forces, and having since committed

mitted

mitted several Murders and mischievous actions.

But it is time to return into *Scotland*, and to see in what posture both Armies are there. The *English*, who would not remain idle, only to keep their Men in action, besieged *Blackness*, a considerable place, and whence their quarters were continually allarum'd by the *Mosse-*Troopers, who retreated and sheltred themselves in that place. Colonel *Monk* commanded in chief in this Expedition, who with but a handfull of men, causing a Battery to be raised, and having given them some few volleys of Cannon, constrained them to yield. On the other side, all the several dissenting parties amongst the Scots, notwithstanding their differences, quarrels, jealousies, and their terrible excommunications, did unite themselves altogether, by their common interest, wherein they concurred to re-establish their King, whereunto they were encouraged by severall under hand practises which were carried on here in *England*, and chiefly in *Lancashire*, which was generally to have risen in Arms: One of the chief Agents interessed in this business, by name Mr. *Thomas Cook*, was taken at *London*, who discovered part of the design, and more was known by Letters which were found in a Vessel sailing from the Mount of *Scotland* to the Isle of *Man*, which belonged to the Earl of *Darby*, and who anon will appear more visibly in this business, as also Mr. *Birkenhead*

We

Blackness taken by Colonel Monk.

The Scots unite.

A Plot discovered.

was taken, being charged with severall Orders and Instructions by which the most hidden and intricate secrets of this conspiracy were discovered. These proceedings obliged the Parliament to order a party both of Horse and Foot under the command of Major General *Harrison*, to march towards the North, as well to dissipate such raisings as should chance to happen there, as to oppose the Enemy, should they make an irruption by the way of *Carlisle*. Meanwhile, several persons of note were impeached, and tryed for having a hand in this Conspiracy : The names of the chief are as followeth, viz. Mr. *Christopher Love*, Major *Alford*, Major *Addams*, Colonel *Barton*, Mr. *Blackmore*, Mr. *Case*, and Mr. *Cawton*, Doctor *Drake*, Mr. *Drake*, Captain *Farr*, Mr. *Gibbons*, Mr. *Haviland*, and Mr. *Jenkins*, Major *Huntington*, Mr. *Jackwell*, Mr. *Jackson*, Mr. *Walton*, Mr. *Robinson*, Captain *Massey*, Captain *Potter*, Lieutenant Colonels, *Jackson*, *Sowton*, and *Vaughan*, and several others.

Two of which number were only put to death, being found more guilty then the rest, to wit, Mr. *Love* and Mr. *Gibbons*, who were both beheaded on *Tower-hill*. And a false report being spread in the principality of *Wales*, that Generall *Cromwell* was defeated in *Scotland*, and that the Royallists Army was entring *England*, a party began to form it self in those parts, but as the cause of the same rising was false, so the effect thereof did soon vanish.

Major General Harrison sent to the North.

Mr. Love & Gibbons beheaded.

Now

Now the *English* being refolved to terminate the warre of *Scotland,* caufed Veffels to be
built, to paffe over the River, and to enter
into *Fife,* which began to allarum the Enemies
who were on the other fide of the water, as alfo
thofe in *Brunts-Ifland.* Nor were the *Scots* idle
neither, but incommodated thofe quarters of
the *English* which were the moft advanced,
which they effected with the greater advantage,
being verfed and known in the wayes and advances, and by this means they flew feveral Englifh Souldiers as they went out to forrage and
to get in Provifions, whereby the English were
conftrained to quit their Out-quarters, and having thus ingroffed their Army by the faid Gar-
rifons, they advanced towards *Fife,* and to that
end made their Magazine at *Blackneffe,* but not
finding wherewithall in the Countrey to feed
their Horfe, they retarded their March for
The Scotch fome few dayes : By which time the Scots ha-
army com- ving compleated their Levies, found them-
pleated re- felves to be 15000 Foot, and 6000 Horfe, with
fufe to which Force they marched toward a place call-
fight. ed *Torwood* on this fide *Sterling,* whereby they
were faced by the English Army, but would not
ingage in a Battail, keeping themfelves within their Bogges, and other inacceffable places,
whereupon the English refolved to paffe over
Colonel part of their Army on the other fide of the
Overton River, and Colonel *Overton* being thereunto
paffes into ordered, did on the 6th of *July,* 1651. paffe
Fife. at *Queens Ferry* with 1600 Foot, and four
Troops

Troops of Horse, having in his said passage lost but six men; as soon as they were arrived they fell to intrenching themselves, and at the same time, the Generall with the body of the Army marched directly towards the Enemy, to the end, that in case the Scots should make a shew to march towards *Fife,* he might charge their Rear, before they should gain *Sterling,* and the Scots being unwilling to let the day passe without driving the English out of *Fife,* sent 4000 Horse and Foot, under the command of Sir *John Brown,* to set upon the English; which obliged Generall *Cromwell* to send over a re-inforcement of two Regiments of Horse, and two Regiments of Foot, under the Command of Major Generall *Lambert,* in lesse then 24 hours they were passed over and joyned to the others, and immediately the Regiment of Colonel *Okey* advanced towards the Enemy, which ingaged them to draw up into Battel-array, and the English likewise did the same, who though they were more in number then the Scots, yet they had the advantage of the ground, and the Scots being placed on a hill, they remained face to face for the space of an hour and a half, looking on each other, the Scots not being willing to march down nor lose their advantage, insomuch that the English at last resolved to march up towards them, and set upon them so resolutely, as that after a very slender contest they quite routed them, and made such a butchery amongst them, that they killed 2000

Major Generall Lambert passes into Fife.

4000 Scots defeated by the English.

2000 of their 4000 took 1400 Prisoners, amongst whom Sir *John Brown* who commanded the Party, Colonel *Buchanan*, and severall other persons of quality on the English side, there were but few slain, but many hurt; and in reference hereunto more Forces were sent over into *Fyfe*, in case the whole Body of both Armies might chance to come to a generall Battell. Immediatly after the English became Masters of *Inchigarvy* a strong Castle, scituate upon a Rock in the midst of the Province of *Fyfe*, between *Queens Ferry* and *North Ferry*, in which there were sixteen piece of Ordnance mounted. On the twenty seventh of *July*, all the English Army appearing before *Brunt Island*, the Governour thereof took such an Alarme thereat, as that after a small Contest in a Parley, he surrendred the same, delivering unto the English, together with the said Island, all the Men of War which were found in the Haven, all the Cannon of the place, as also all the Armes, Ammunition of War, and the provision of Victuals; which said Isle was very considerable for the English to make a Magazine and Storehouse for the Provisions and Ammunition for the Army.

Brunt Island surrendred.

Thence the Army marched to *St. John's Town*, a very strong and considerable place, into which the Enemy had but just before put a fresh Regiment, who were resolved to have defended themselves very well, but as soon as they saw that their Sluces were cut off by the English, they lost their Courage, and surrendred the place, Mean-

St. Johns Town surrendred.

Meanwhile there happened a great change of Affairs, for the Scots Army consisting in 16000 men, abandoned their own Territories, in hopes of establishing themselves in a better Country, and by the way of *Carlisle* enter *England*.

General *Cromwell* being advertised hereof, issued out immediatly such Orders as were requisite to pursue the Scots, and with all possible speed the Army repassed the River of *Fife* upon a Bridge of Boats at *Leith*, Major General *Lambert* the sooner to overtake the Enemies Rear, with 3000 Horse and Dragoons followed after them, and Major General *Harrison* with a Body of lighter Horse, was commanded to get into the Van of the Enemy, for to amuse and detain them, whilst the General himself with the Body of the Army consisting in sixteen Regiments of Horse and Foot immediatly pursued the Enemy.

But not wholly to abandon the Affaires of *Scotland*; Colonel Monk was left there with 7000 men, with which alone he perfected the Conquest of that *Kingdome*, taking immediatly after this Change of the *Scene*, the strong Town and Castle of *Sterling* being a very considerable Place, and also *Aberdeen*, *Dundee*, and the strong Castle of *Dunnotters*, and *Dunbarton*, with many others: Insomuch, as that after the passage into *Fyfe* was once gained, the remaining parts of *Scotland* were soon entirely subdued, and were made tributary unto the Common-wealth of *England*.

Mean

Mean while, the divided Parties of the English
Forces which pursued the *Scots* Army, did quite
and clean tire them out during their March; setting upon them sometimes in the Van, sometimes in the Rear, sometimes in the Flank; and
finally, on all sides as they saw their oportunity
to disturb and annoy them: Insomuch that their
long and precipitated March did much weaken
the *Scots.* But that which troubled and vexed
them most of all, was the little hopes they saw
of those promises of relief which were given
them from *England,* The Parliament having
settled such good Orders in all parts, as that no
body durst stir or rise in Armes to their Aide. In
all places wheresoever the Scots came they
proclaimed their King, To be King of great
Britain, France, and *Ireland,* according to the
accustomed Formes; and in his Name they sent
unto all those who had any Commands, or were
in any Authority in those parts through which
they passed, to rise in Armes joyntly with them,
but no body budged. To the contrary by Order of Parliament the Trained Bands of severall
Countries drew forth in Armes, to hinder the
Risings, and to augment the Common-wealths
Armies. On the one side, General *Cromwells*
Army marched on the Heels of the Scots to
their Terrour; on the other side, the Major General *Lambert* and *Harrison* waited upon their
Designs, and Colonel *Robert Lilborn* was left in
Lancashire, to hinder the Earl of *Darby* from
levying men in those parts, and to the same
purpose

purpose, severall other Bodies were placed in other places, as the occasion required, both to cut off the Enemies Provisions, as well as his passage ; In case they should resolve to retreat back again, or to fly away.　Finally, the *Scotch* Army having reached the Town of *Worcester*, pitched its Camp there, having much debated where, and in what manner they should fix upon a resting and breathing place, after so long and tedious a march : Whereof the Earl of *Darby* was no sooner assertained, but he issued forth of his Island with 300 Gentlemen, and Landed in *Lancashire*, where he assembled at least 1200 men, during which, the Generals Regiment which was left at *Manchester*, was Commanded to joyn with Colonel *Lilborne*, to cut off the Earl of *Darbies* passage to *Manchester*, whither he was marching to have faln upon the said Regiment ; but Colonel *Lilborne* observing his motion, marched the very same way, joyning Flank and Flank, with the Earls Forces, who deeming that he ought not to defer the Fight with *Lilborne*, till he should have joyned with the Generals Regiment, when as then he might have proved too strong, but whilst he was weaker being alone, fell upon Colonel *Lilborne*, and each side for the space of four hours fight did behave themselves very well, till at length the Earls Forces being worsted, he was constrained to save himself, and to gain *Worcester*, almost all alone ; amongst Prisoners of note, which were taken in this Encounter, were Colonel *Legg*, *Robinson*,

The Earle of *Darby* defeated.

Robinson, Baines, Gerrard, four Livetenant Colonels, one Major, four Captains, two Livetenants, twenty Gentlemen, and five hundred Soldiers. There were killed the Lord *Withrinton,* Sir *Thomas Fieldsley,* Colonel *Boynton,* Sir *William Throgmorton,* Sir   *Gamwell,* and sixty Soldiers.

On the Parliaments side there were but ten men slain, but abundance were hurt, which defeat, although it was but a small one, yet it was very ominous, and served not a little to discourage those who were on the Brink of declining themselves, and ready to rise in Armes, so that it may be said without vanity, that the defeating of those 1500 men, hindred above 10000 to joyn with the *Scots* at *Worcester* : and indeed Colonel *Lilborne* received those Honours and that recompense from the Parliament which was due to his Valour; And the Lord General *Cromwell* whose prudence did at all times equallize his Valour, nay far surpass it, being conscious that diligence and expedition was more then requisite in this Conjuncture, which was like unto a Gangren, continually gaining ground, and therefore immediatly to be cut off, least it should endanger the whole, arived with his Army at *Worcester,* sooner then he was expected, with a resolution to make his Enemies either perish within the place, or constrain them to give Battel. Here War-like Stratagems or wiles were not necessary, for there was no delaying of the businesse, neither was there

there any retreat to be made, or flight to be taken; It matters not for one Town more or less, This is the upshot Blow, where the best Swords were, to decide the Interest of three Crowns. The Royallists were backed by dispaire, and the others were animated with the continuall and accustomed defeating of their Enemies; Now both must either fight or die, and resolve to be a Cast or nothing, and the Town of *Worcester,* this very day must be the bloody *Theater,* of the fairest chance of Fortune which ever happened in the Isles of great *Brittain*; The first thing therefore which the Parliaments Forces endeavoured, was to gain a pass over the River of *Severne,* which was immediatly performed by Major Generall *Lambert,* at a place called *Upton,* and which passage was made good by Lieutenant Generall *Fleetwoods* Brigade, which advancing towards *Tame River,* a Bridge of Boats was laid over the same, and likewise another Bridge was made over *Stoure* on the Generals side, which being perceived by the Royallists they caused a Body both of Horse and Foot to advance to oppose the Lieutenant Generals passage, who was backed by two Regiments of Foot of Colonel *Inglesbies,* and Colonel *Fairfax's,* by the Generals Troops of Guard, and Colonel *Blackers* Regiment of Horse, all which were animated and encouraged by the Generals presence, who marched at the Head of them, after which Colonel *Goffs,* and Major Generall *Deans* Regiments were passed over the River, who began

to scoure the Hedges which were lined by the
Enemy, and whence they drave them away,
beating them from Hedge to Hedge, being sup-
plyed with fresh men, but after this kind of Skir-
mish had lasted well nigh a good hour, very
smartly, the Royallists were constrained to give
ground, and to retire to *Powick* Bridge; which
they made good for an hour longer, but quitting
it at length, they retired toward the Town, except those which were made Prisoners; and
within a little while afterwards, having assembled all their Forces, and all their Courage to
boot, they issued forth of the Town in a Body
towards the Generals side, believing that the
best part of his Army had been on the other side
(as in effect it was seperated in two by the a-
fore specified River, and the Royallists at their
first charge were so furious and resolute, as that
the Generals Troops were constrained to give
way, but that only served to augment their courage, and make them more covetous of Glory:
Insomuch, that renewing their Fight with a fresh
vigour, they charged the Enemy so impetuously, as that the *Scotch* Army both Horse and Foot
were on a suddain over borne and quite brought
into disorder, all their Works and Lynes, together with their Royall Fort, and their Cannon
were immediatly taken, and turned upon and a-
gainst themselves; the Town was given in Pil-
lage, and all their Foot were either slain or taken Prisoners, a Body of 3000 Horse brake
through and made their escape, and one thousand

*The Scots
defeated
at Worce-
ster.*

and of them were taken by Colonel *Barton* who lay about *Bemdly*, only with a few Horse and Dragoons, and Colonel *Lilborne* with the Generals Regiments of Foot accidentally met with the Earl of *Darby*, who a little before had escaped him, whom he seized, together with the Earl of *Landerdale*, and above a hundred persons of quality, severall others were likewise taken by the other parties which were abroad; as Duke *Hamilton* General of the *Scotch* Army, who afterwards died of his Wounds, the Earl of *Rothe*, the Earl of *Cornwarth*, the Earle of *Shrewsbury*, *Packington*, *Cunningham*, and *Clare*, Knights, the Lords *Spine* and *Sinclere*, the Earle of *Cleaveland*, of *Kelley*, and Colonel *Greaves*, six Colonels of Horse, thirteen of Foot, nine Lieutenant Colonels of Horse, eight of Foot, six Majors of Horse, thirteen of Foot, thirty seven Captains of Horse, seventy three of Foot, fifty five Quarter-masters, eighty nine Lieutenants of Foot, Major Generall *Biscotty*, Major General *Montgomery*, the Lieutenant General of the Ordnance, the adjutant General of the Foot, the Martiall General, the Quarter-master General, the Conductor General of the Baggage, seventy six Standards, ninety nine Ensigns, nine Ministers, nine Chirurgions, one hundred fifty eight Colours, and all the Cannon, and Baggage generally, the Royall Standard, the Kings Coach and Horses, the Royall Robe, the Collar of the Order of the Garter, thirty of his domestick Servants, and his Secretary *Fanshaw*,

H   as

as for the King his own person, he made and escaped strangely, and in a disguise he saved himself at length into *France*, not without many difficulties and dangers; Notwithstanding the Parliament had promised five hundred pounds to any one that could discover his Person. Several other persons were also afterwards taken in the remotest Countries, as Major General *Massey*, who afterwards made an escape, Major General *Middleton*, Livetenant General *David Lesly*, and severall others; insomuch, as that it may be said, the Gleanings of this Victory, were as considerable as the whole Harvest it self.

But let us return to our CONQUEROR, and observe with what a moderation he enjoyed this his Victory, he desires no triumphall preparations, He would not that thanks should be returned to him for the same; but only to God alone, who helped him with his mighty Arme to advance his own Glory, and to establish the peace and repose of *England*, upon solid and firm Foundations, and when as the Parliament did propound unto him most splendid and magnificent Presents, in recompense, he only desired the Lives and Liberties of their Prisoners. They proposed to have Bonefires made, and to have Triumphall Arcks erected, but he answered, That it would be better to raise Monuments to such of their Illustrious Patriots as lost their lives in the gaining of that Day, and to bewaile their deaths with Tears. And lastly at the Generalls request, these were onely the Earle of
Darby,

Darby, and Sir *Fetherston* Knight, of all this great number of Prisoners put to death, besides some few others of less quality.

Much about which time also, that smal Body of an Army which remained in *Scotland*, seized upon a great number of the Nobility of the Country, who were assembled all together at a place called *Elles*, where the old General *Lefly*, Earle *Marshall*, the Lord *Keith*, *Cofford*, *Ogleby*, *Barmy*, *Huntly*, *Lee*, and severall other Knights, Gentlemen, and Ministers, were in Consultation, all of which were put on boord a Ship, and sent into *England*.

The remaining Nobility of *Scotland* seised and sent into *England*.

This great Storm being thus over-blown, and the Minds of the Parliament Members being calmed, after the apprehensions of the Scotch Invasion, and the doubtfull and unexpected Events of a Battel, they began to track the Footsteps of their Conquest a new, and the whole Common-wealth being entirely cleansed within, they cast about how to reduce those Islands which sheltred several of the Enemies smal Vessels, whereby the Trade was interrupted, and several Merchant-men impeded in their Voyages: The Isle of *Jersey* was the first they resolved to begin withall, and the Conduct of this Enterprise was left to Colonel *Haynes*, who upon the same accompt on the fourteenth of *October*, 1651. caused two Regiments of Foot, and as many of Horse to be embarqued on board of eight Ships, in the Port of *Weymouth*, and the seventeenth they set Saile, but the stormy Weather

The Isle of *Jersey* attempted

forced

forced them to return : On the nineteenth they
set saile again, and on the same day about Midnight, they came to anchor under the Island
of *Zeark*, and next Morning continuing their
Course, they arived at *Stowens Bay* in *Jersey*; on
the next day they fell down with the Tyde, and
got into St. *Brelads* Bay, where they were assailed by so vehement a storm, as that the Fleet
was dispersed, but having joyned to each other
again ; on the one and twentieth they resolved
to go ashoare that Night at *Stowens* Bay, whereunto they were necessitated for want of Forrage
for the Horse, and as it were in a trice, they
landed their Horse by an admirable Industry of
General *Blake*, and his other Officers in Boats,
and two hours after the Flood they weighed
anchor, and some cut their Cables to run a
shoare, and so the Foot Landed some at three
some at four, some at five, and some at six foot
set and more, receiving all that while both the
Cannon and Musket shot which played upon
them from the shoare ; Notwithstanding which
they gained Land, although they were faced by
both the Horse and Foot of the Island, but this
was their advantage, they were so over-charged
with Water, as that they were not succeptible
of Fire. Finally, after they had endured this
first brunt, they got all of them on shoare, and
quickly gained as much Ground as served them
to draw up into a Body to fight, which they accordingly did, with so much resolution and vigour, that in one half houres time they forced
the

the Enemy to retreat, who left their Enſignes behind them, and twelve piece of Cannon, after which the Horſe being a little hearmed having been refreſhed in their Quarters in the Iſland, on the two and twentieth of *October* they attempted three ſmall Forts, each having two piece of Ordnance in them which they took, after which, they advanced within ſight of *Elizabeths* Caſtle, to ſet upon a Fort called the Tower of St. *Albans*, having fourteen piece of Ordnance commanded by the ſaid Caſtle : In two hours time they gained the ſaid Tower, and their next work was to poſſeſs the Caſtle of *Montorqueil*, which they alſo took without much trouble ; But *Elizabeths* Caſtle being a very ſtrong and conſiderable place into which they had retired all their Forces, was not ſurrendred untill the midſt of the Month of *December*, on the moſt advantagious Conditions which ſo conſiderable a place could expect. *Jerſey and all the Caſtles taken.*

On the ſixteenth of *October* 1651. there were embarqued at *Weſtcheſter* and *Leverpoole* three Regiments of Foot, to wit, General *Cromwells*, commanded by Livetenant Colonel *Worſly*, Major General *Deanes* Commanded by Livetenant Colonel *Michell*, and Colonel *Duckinfields*, who Commanded the whole Brigade, together with two Troops of Horſe, which Forces were ſent to reduce the Iſle of *Man*. *The Iſle of Man attempted, and reduced.*

On the eighteenth of the ſaid Month they ſet Sail, but the VVind coming contrary, they were driven into the Port of *Beaumorris*. On the

H 3   twenty

twenty fifth, by two in the Morning the Wind coming Southwardly, by the favour of a fresh Gale, they set Sail again, and about two of the Clock in the Afternoon they discovered the Castle of the Isle of *Man*, *Rushen* Castle, *Darby* Fort, and a good part of the Island, as also the Inhabitants and Soldiery, as well Horse and Foot in Armes, who were drawn out to make a review of their Forces, when as by a suddain Gust the Fleet was hindred from approaching neerer the shoare, whereupon they tacked about towards the North of the Island, and not without some difficulty they gained *Ramsey* Bay, where they Anchored that Night in sight of the Island, and sent them Volleys of Cannon which were not at all answered by those of the Island.   On the twenty sixth of *October*, an Inhabitant was sent on board the Fleet from the chief persons of the Island, to assure the Commander that they would not in any wise hinder their Landing, But to the contrary that they would deliver up unto them two Forts which they had Mastered, after which there remained only *Rushen* and *Peele* Castle to be taken, wherein they would also be assisting to the utmost of their powers: But because the said Inhabitant brought nothing in writing to confirm what he had said, Major *Fox* went on shoare to be assured of the certainty thereof, and returning well satisfied, he was followed by some Commissioners of the Island, who most humbly beseeched the Officers not to ruine them, which must of necessity

necessity enforce, should they Land all their Men,
obliging and engaging themselves to bring Provisions at reasonable rates, unto those who
should remain on board the Ships: The Commander in chief returned them thanks, promising them to do them all the favour possible and
imaginable; but it fell out unhappily for all
sides: That on the twenty seventh the Sea became very rough, and the Ships being not able
to remain all of them under shelter in the said
Bay, they were in a great deal of danger, and
one Ship running ashoare, was broken and rent
in sunder; however all the men were saved, and
those within the Castles knowing full well the
danger wherein the Ships were, did encrease the
dangers from shoare as well as from Sea, and
thereby became the more resolute and obstinate; Insomuch that on the twenty eighth they
were constrained to Land the Horse and the rest
of the Foot, who became Masters of the Forts,
and afterwards set upon the Castles, in one of
which was the Earle of *Darbies* Widow, who
quickly surrendred herself, together with all the
Ammunitions of War, and some Vessells which
were Anchored in the Harbour.

And not long after the strong Castle of *Guern-*
sey was also surrendred to the Parliament, the
whole Island having alwaies remained under the
obedience of the Common-wealth, and never
deserted the same.

And, as there is no felicity on this under the
Heavens, which is not mingled with some bit-

Guernsey Castle surrendred.

ter

terness; so in like manner, the great Conquest of the Parliament both by Sea and Land, had some mixture of misfortunes on both Elements, on the Land by the decease of a great Captain, and a greater States-man, and on the Sea by the death of a great Pilot, and a greater Admirall both together.   The first was the Lord *Ireton*, Son-in-law to his late Highness, who immediatly after the taking of *Limrick*, a very considerable place in those parts, died, during his being Lord Deputy of *Ireland*, he was generally bemoaned of all men, being a person who had rendred himself equally famous in War-like Exploits, as well as in Politick Affairs, and Sagacious Councels, and to speak the truth, there was scarce his like in all *England*, and all the Comforts which survived his loss, were, that those good Foundations which he had laid, and the Maximes which he had prescribed for the Government of *Ireland* did not perish with him, but have remained to his Successors, as Lamps and Lights whereby they may safely conduct their Foot-steps, and assuredly carry on their Designes.

The other famous Person who also dyed, was General *Popham*, a Personage endowed with all the good qualities of an exquisite Sea-man, being valiant, active, and well versed in Sea Affaires, his precipitated death, and the small time he continued in that Imployment, did shew unto us less what he was, then according unto all appearance what he would have been, had it pleased

pleased God to have lengthned his daies. And now the Parliament being truly sencible both of the old and new Injuries which *England* had received from, and by the States of *Holland,* thought it fit to publish this ensuing Manifest; *Vic.*

THat no Commodities whatsoever of the growth or Manufacture of *Africa, Asia, America,* or *Europe,* should be brought into *England,* or into any of the Territories belonging thereunto, either by the English themselves, or by any others, save in Vessels, or Barques, effectively belonging to this Common-wealth, or the Collonies and Plantations in the *Indies,* who depend on the same, on the penalty of forfeiting both Ships and Goods.

2. That all Commodities whatsoever of the growth or manifacture of Forreigners which shall be brought within the Dominions of this Common-wealth, in Vessels belonging to the Inhabitants thereof shall be taken and laden only in the places where the said wares do grow or else in those Ports and Havens, whence they must of necessity be brought, and where they are accustomed to be had and bought at the first hand.

3. That all kind of Fish of the Fishing belonging to the people of this Nation, as also all kind of Oyle of Fish, VVhales Oyle,

An Act of Parliament, concerning the Importation and exportation of Goods & Merchandises.

Oyle, and VVhale Bones, shall not be brought, save in such Ships where the said Fishing shall have been made, upon the forementioned Penalty.

4. That after the first of *February,* 1653. there shall be no Salt-fish transported out of *England,* save in English Vessels, &c. Then which nothing was more pleasing to the Merchants, nor could any thing have more encouraged them, to cause the Traffick and Navigation to flourish again, and whereby they were not a little endeared to the Parliaments Interest: So likewise was it very effectual to gain the Seamens hearts, then which nothing is so apt to rebellion and so hard to be kept in awe.

So likewise several other Ordinances and Regulations were made concerning those Merchandizes which are brought from the *East Indies,* from the *Levant,* and from the Coast of *Spain* and *Portugal;* all which did not much please, and but little oblige the Hollanders; but to the contrary did so exasperate their Minds, as that even during the time when they were treating of an Accommodation, it came to an open VVar, concerning the point of Honour or Seas, and in this wise the Quarrel began.

A Rupture with *Holland* caused.

The first Sea-fight with the *Hollander,* *May* 52.

MAjor *Bourn* Commander in chief of a Squadron of English Ships, discovered *Van Trump* Admiral of the Dutch Fleet, on the back of *Goodwine Sands,* who with two and forty Saile

Saile of Ships made towards *Dover Road*, whereupon the Frigat called the *Greyhound* was commanded to make all the possible saile she could
after them, to speak with them, which she accordingly did, whereas they struck their
Saile, and gave all kind of tokens of honour and
respect, saying moreover, That they would
gladly tell something in the behalf of their Admiral, unto the Party that commanded the English Fleet in chief, and coming on board, they
saluted the English Ships, and to seem the more
officious, they gave them an Account of their
Navigation in this wise; saying, That the No-
thernly VVinds having been somewhat high for
some daies, they had been constrained to ply
more to the Southward, then else they willing-
ly would have done, and that being come to an
Anchor somewhat hitherwards, to avoid the falling too neer unto *Dunkirk*, they had lost severall Cables and Anchors, concluding that they
had not the least intention to do us any Injury.
General *Blake* was at that time with the rest of
the Fleet towards the VVest, who being en-
formed by Major *Bourn* of the Hollanders proceedings, he used all the possible speed he could
to joyne with him, and on the nineteenth of
May he discovered the Hollanders Anchored in
Dover Road, and being within three Leagues of
each other, the Hollander weighed Anchor, and
sailed Eastward, where they met with an Express from the States, whom they spake withall,
and afterwards made all the Saile they could up
to

to the English Fleet, their Admiral *Van Trump*
shewing himself upon the Decks of the foremost Ships ; And General *Blake* coveting the
honour to give the first Volley, let fly three
Guns at *Van Trumps* Flag, though without Bullets , To which *Van Trump* answered by a shot
from the Stern of his Ship backwards, signifying
his disdain to vale his Flag, and instead of the
striking his Main Top-Saile, he caused a red
Flag of War to be set up, in token of a Combat
to his whole Fleet, and without any further delay, he gave General *Blake* a whole Broad-side,
who joyfully received it, and returned two for
one, and for the space of foure houres together
both Fleets fought with that Animosity and vehemency, which is usually on the like occasions
at the first fallings out : when at last, having severall times past and repast through and through
each other, General *Blake* obtained the Victory,
having sunk one *Holland* Man of War , took
another with thirty Guns made a hundred and
fifty Prisoners, and both the Captains of the
said Ships, and sent the rest of their Fleet home
by weeping Cross, to tell the rest of their But-
ter-box Brethren the success of their rash Attempt : The English lost but ten Men in this
Fight, and had forty wounded, and of the
whole Fleet, the Generals Ship alone was somewhat endamaged in her Masts, Sails, Tackling,
and Apparel ; After which the States of *Holland*
disowned and disavowed this Action, and to
that purpose sent over two extraordinary Ambassadors

sadors into *England*, who represented these
Reasons to the Parliament of *England*, therein
declaring, *Viz.*

That the unhappy Fight betwixt the Fleets
of both Common-wealths, hapned without
their knowledge, and contrary to the will and
desire of the Lords, the States General of the
united Provinces, taking God to witness of
this Truth, who knows the hearts of men, and
that both by Letters and Messages they had continually been assured of the said Lords and
States Sincerity : That with astonishment and
amazement they had received the fatall tydings
of so rash an Attempt and Action; and that immediatly they entred into Consultation, how
they might best find out a remedy to soften and
excuse this fresh bleeding Wound: To which
end they had convocated a general Assembly of
the Provinces, in the which they doubted not,
God willing, to meet with a present remedy to
these Troubles, whereby not only the Causes
of all the evils which might ensue, should
be removed, but also by an interiour Comfort
mens Minds might be rectified, and brought to a
better hope of the Treaty which was on Foot,
wherein their Lordships laboured daily, and in
good earnest for the Welfare of both Nations,
to avoid the further effusion of Christian blood,
so much desired by the Enemies unto both Nations; wherefore they requested and desired
most humbly of this honourable Councel by the
Pledges of the Liberty and their mutuall con-
currence

currence in Religion ; Not to suffer any
thing to be undertaken with too much precipitation and heat, which might at length become
irrevocable, and not to be remedied by vaine
Wishes, or too late Vows; but that without
delay they might receive a favourable Answer,
which they the more earnestly desire, since their
Lordships , the States Ships , and Marriners
were detained and impeded in their Voyages,
some by force and others by the Fights at Sea,
and the rest in the Ports of this Common-
Wealth.

Whereunto the Parliament thus replyed,
Viz.

THat whereas they remember with what
continual Demonstrations of Friendship
they alwaies Comported themselves towards
their Neighbours of the united Provinces, ever
since the beginning of their Civil Wars, having
not omitted any thing which might tend to the
preservation of a good understanding betwixt
them, they think it very strange to find how ill
the said States have answered these their Civilities, and especially by the Acts of Hostilitie
which they have lately exercised against this
Common-wealths Fleet, and having taken the
whole into their Consideration, as well as the
severall Papers presented to the Council of
State by their Ambassadors; They do thereon
answer, That as they are ready to give a favourable

the interpretation to the expressions contained in the said Papers, tending to represent how that the last Fight which happned lately, was without the knowledge, and contrary to the intentions of their Masters; so likewise, when they consider how incomformable and inconsistent with these Thoughts and Discourses the proceedings of their State, and the behaviour of their Sea-men hath been in the very midst of a Treaty, and in what a manner the said particulars have been Negotiated here by their Ambassador; The extraordinary preparations of a 156 Ships without any apparent necessity, and the Instructions which were by the said Lords States given to the Sea-men, we have but too great cause to believe, That the Lords the States General of the united Provinces, have a design to usurp the known right which the English have to the Seas, To destroy their Fleets, which after God, are their Walls and Bulwarks, and thereby to expose the Common-wealth to an Invasion, according to their own good liking, even as they have attempted to do by their last Action : whereupon the Parliament do think themselves to be obliged, to endeavour by Gods assistance, as they shall find occasion for the same, to seek the reparation of those Wrongs which they have already received, and an assurance for the future against the like which might be attempted against them : However with a desire and an intention that things may be composed and put up in an amicable way, if it be possible by such waies and means as God by his Providence shall Lay open, and by such circumstances as may tend to hasten this Designe, and may render it more efficacious then any other of the like nature hath not yet been.

Open War with Holland. So that this Conference besides many others, having not been caple to produce the Agreement and expected Reconciliation; the *Holland* Ambassadors took their leaves of the Parliament, by a publick Audience, and went their ways. And immediatly both these powerful Common-wealths prepared for an open VVar, all the Waters of the Ocean being not able to quench their just Indignations, and those Forces which they will both engender upon the Surface of the Sea, may well and duly represent unto us the Image of the Chaos, and the VVars of the Elements.

The Hollanders Fishermen destroyed in the North. General *Blake* who seemed to have fastned the Saile of Fortune to his most prodigious mast by the glorious appearance of his gallant and resolute Fleet, makes Saile towards the Northen Parts, and about the Isles of *Orkney*, and seised upon all the *Holland* Vessels which he found Fishing on that Coast, most part of the Fishing Barques he sent away, and discharged as unworthy Objects, or Ornaments to so state-

ly

ly a Navall Armado; but the twelve *Holland* Men of War which were to convoy and secure them, he brought home with him.

On the other side, Sir *George Askue* remaining in the Channel with another Squadron of Ships, to clear and guard the same, discovered thirty Saile of *Hollanders* betwixt *Callis* and *Dover*, to which he gave Chace, and constrained them all for the most part to run a shoare on the Coast of *France*, onely ten excepted, which were taken, burnt, and sunck, and in reference to this fatall Rupture, there was not a day past wherin Prizes were not made by the English on the *Hollander* and *French*, who likewise were not as yet well reconciled to the *English*.

A Holland Fleet destroyed by Sir *Geo. Askue.*

Thence Sir *George Askue* set Saile towards the West, as well to seek out for the *Hollander*, as to guard those Coasts, and to convoy the Merchant-Men which were ready to set Saile from *Plimouth* through the Channel, and being come within seven or eight Leagues of the said Port, he had notice given him that the *Holland* Fleet was not far off, whereupon calling a Councel of Warre, it was conceived they might be met with about the Coast of *France*, a Resolution was taken to make Saile thither-

I

wards

wards ; and the same day which was the sixteenth of *August* , betwixt one and two of the Clock in the Afternoon they discovered the *Holland* Fleet, and immediatly made up towards them as fast as they could , and found them to be sixty Men of Warre , and thirty Merchant men ; the English were but eight and thirty Men of Warre , foure Fire Ships , and foure small Frigats , who notwithstanding the inequalitie of of their Number , about foure of the Clock of the said Afternoon , encountred the Enemy with as much Gallantry and Resolution as possible could be expected.

The *Plimouth* fight with the Dutch. And Sir *George Askue* seconded by six other Ships immediatly Charged into the very Body of the Enemy , and however they were sufficiently damaged by this first Charge, in their Sailes Masts, and Yards , yet they got to the Wind-ward of their Enemies , and once againe Charged the whole Body of them , continuing their said Combat very fiercely in this wise , and alwayes being intermingled pell-mell with the Enemy , untill the obscurnesse of the Night had seperated them, and had the rest of the Fleet imployed their parts as well as Sir *George Askue's* Squadron did , it is believed the whole *Hollands* Fleet

Fleet had been destroyed : amongst the
English there were severall hurt and killed , however but one Person of Note,
Captaine *Pack* a Person of Honour ,
and a very Valiant , stout , and experienced Sea-man , whose Legg being shot
off by a Cannon Bullet , he died immediatly ; there were also two other
Captaines hurt , *Viz. Little* , and *Whi-
teridge* , Two of the *Holland* Men of
Warre , and one of their Fire Ships
were sunck , as might be guest by the
Wrecks afterwards ; for the Night which
terminated this Fight , did also debarre
the sight of the Fleets what it had produced : So that the *Hollanders* continued their Course towards the Coast of
France , and the *English* towards *Plimouth* , to repaire their Vessels , but
especially their Masts , Yards , and Tackling , which were so much endamaged ,
that they were forced to give over the
pursuite of the Enemy.

And much about the same time that
this Fight happened , Generall *Blake*
steering North-wards , took six *Holland*
Ships of a great value about the *Downes* ,
and sent one Frigat toward the East , to
re-inforce Sir *George Askue* ; presently afterwards Captaine *Penne* plying also upon the Coast of *France* , took six *Holland* Ships , which had formerly been

Six Hollanders Ships taken by Gen. Blake.

Six more ta-ken by Cap-tain Penne.

in the *Venetian* Service, and were all of them bound homewards richly Laden, being all Men of Warre of considerable Burthen.

A French Fleet taken by Gen. Blake.

On the fifth of *September*, General *Blakes* Fleet riding at Anchor in the *Downes*, having notice that a *French* Fleet was to touch in *Callis* Road, there to take both Men and Ammunition on Boord for the Reliefe of *Dunkirk*, he weighed Anchor, and made towards them, and about five in the Evening they were riding it out of *Callis* Road, with a Designe in the Night to have set Saile towards *Dunkirk* : But General *Blake* as soon as they were got to Sea gave them Chace, and pursued them to the very Flats before *Dunkirk*, as farre as he durst, by reason of the Flats, and the Burthen of his Ships ; he took seven of their Men of Warre, the least carrying two and twenty Guns, and one Frigat with eight Guns, and also one of their Fire Ships ; whereupon the Garrison of *Dunkirk* having been disappointed of their expected Reliefe of Ammunition and Provisions : Not long after was forced, together with the rest of the Garrisons which depended on the same, to yield to the *Spaniards*.

On the twenty seventh of *September*, General *Blake* discovered about sixty Saile of *Holland* Men of Warre, Commanded

ded by Admiral *Dewit*, on the back-side
of the *Goodwin* Sands, so that next day
he set Saile and made towards the Enemy, but falling upon a Flat called the
Kentish Knock (under which the *Hol-*
lander had purposely sheltred themselves,
to endanger the *English*, should they attempt to gain the Windward of them) they
found they had but three Fathome Water, so that severall of the Fleet struck
upon the Sands, but had no other harme,
which caused them to stand off againe,
and to make directly towards the Enemy, endeavouring to engage them to a
Fight : But the *Hollander* being unwilling
to engage, all that day past in slight Skirmishes onely, towards Evening the *Hol-*
landers changed their Station, but kept
themselves off from the *English* towards
the Flats, making a shew of being desirous to fight : But the next Morning by
break of day, the English Fleet perceiving
that the *Hollanders* were gone about two
Leagues Northward from them, they resolved although they had but very little
Wind, and that various to make up towards them, which they endeavoured all
the Morning, but could not reach them,
the Wind being come North, inclined to
the West : However the best Sailing Frigats were commanded to make after them,
and to keep them in play till the rest of

The Ken ih
Knock, a fight
with the Hol-
landers.

I 3   the

the Fleet could get up to them, and about
three in the Afternoon, the said Frigats
with much add got within shot of them,
but the *Hollander* fearing least by degrees
they might be drawn to a generall Combat (as it indeed was the *English*'s, Designe) hoyst up their maine Top-failes,
and fairely run away ; Notwithstanding
which, ten good Frigats gave the Chace,
till ten at Night, and the next Morning by
the favour of a fresh Gale from the South-
west, the whole Fleet pursued them till
they came to *West Cappell* in *Zeland*, when
as they put into *Gore*, the English would
faine have falne on and fought them in
their own Ports, but a Councel of Warre
being called, it was judged unfitting to
pursue them any further upon their owne
Coasts, by reason of the *Flats*, and also
by reason that the *English* Provisions began to fall short: The *Hollanders* loss in
this Encounter is not well known, that
which was visible was, that three of their
Ships were disenabled from fighting, the
one having her Main-mast shot downe, and
the Mizen-mast, Bowsprits, Staies and
Tackling of the other two ; the Admiral
of their Reare Squadron was reduced to
so ill a plight, as being not able to make
any way of her self, they were constrained
to tow her a long by a Hoy of two and
thirty great Guns , which advanced but
flowly

flowly forward: fo that the *Nonefuch* Frigat boarded her, and having put thirty men over into each Veffell, they maftered them, but finding that they were extream leakie, and began to finck, they took eighty men out of them, and their Officers, the Reare Admiral, and the Captaine, and left the Hulks to ferve the dead men for a Coffin: The *Englifh* had but forty men killed, and as many hurt. Now the fame of this notable Warre between thefe two Queenly and Miftrefs Common-wealths of the Navigation, having fpread it felf throughout the Univerfe in all places, where Trade and Commerce is ufed; The eftects thereof appeared fhortly after in the Mediterranian Seas, as well as in the Ocean and in the *Englifh* Channel: Some Frigats were fent towards the *Levant*, to guard the *Englifh* Merchant Men from the *French* Shipping of *Marfelleis*, and *Toulon*, a Squadron of which Frigats confifting onely in foue Saile of Ships, *viz.* The *Paragon*, the *Phenix*, the *Conftant Warwick*, and the *Elizabeth*, convoying three Merchant Men, two of which had taken in their Lading at *Scandaroon*, and the other at *Smyrna*, were encountred by eleven *Holland* Men of War, who made up towards them, and fet upon them; All that the *Englifh* could at firft do, was to returne their broad Sides on

I 4 their

their Poopes, to let them see that they were not affraid of their exceeding them in number, but ere the fight was well begun, the Night sephrated them, and the next Morning the *Hollanders* began the fight againe, and were received as briskly, as if they had been equally matched. The Masts and Yards of two of their Ships were quickly shot downe, and another was set on fire, but quickly recovered; The *Phenix* a gallant Frigat of five and forty Guns was boarded by a huge States Ship, and after a marvellous defence lost almost all her Men (and being over powerd) was forced to yield, but not without a great loss on the *Hollanders* side; Nor did the *English* quit the fight till all their Men and Ammunition were killed and spent: The *Paragon* lost seven and twenty Men, and had sixty wounded, the *Elizabeth* had but two Barrels of Powder left; However they disengaged themselves from so great a number of their Enemies, and put their Merchant-men safe in *Porto longone*; So that the *Hollander* had not much to brag of in the fight which hapned neer *Corsica.* Much about this time an Ambassador from the Queen of *Sweden;* but before he had made the least overture of Business, he dyed: Another Ambassador arrived from the King of *Denmark*, but finding

Two Ambassadors arrive in *England.*

finding that it was impossible to reconcile
the differences betwixt the two Common-
wealths, he withdrew againe and went his
wayes, by reason of the common Interest
of the *Danes*, and the united Provinces :
And the Parliament having notice that
the *Hollanders* who blocked up the passage
of the *Sound*, had constrained two and
twenty *English* Merchants coming from
the Eastern Parts towards *England*, to
put themselves under the King of *Denmark*, protection, ordered eighteen Saile
of Ships to go to fetch them home, the rather because they were Laden with such
Merchandizes, as were at that time very
usefull for the State, and without which
the Warre against the *Hollanders* could not
be prosecuted nor continued.

On the nineteenth of *September*, the
Fleet set saile from *Yarmouth*, and the next
Morning they came to Anchor within two
Leagues of the Castle of *Essenboeur*, in *Denmark*, whence the Commander in chief sent
away the *Greyhound* Frigat, with a Letter
directed to the Governour of the Castle,
and another to the Admiral of *Denmark*,
by which he desired them to informe the
King of *Denmark* of their arrivall, and of
the Subject thereof, whereunto he added a third Letter, directed to the Masters
of the *English* Ships, ordering them to
make

Severall passa-
ges between
the English &
the Danes.

make their Addresses to the King of *Den-*
mark, and to procure libertie from him
that their Ships might with all speed be
suffered to come out of the   of *Co-*
penhagen, where they as then lay : But the
Frigat was not suffered to approach neerer
then within a League of the Castle ,
whence she returned againe. The next
Morning the Commander in Chief himselfe went thither in his long Boat , and
declared the Subject of his Arrivall , and
delivered his Letters, but no Answer was
returned unto him, which obliged him
the second time to send to the King,
and to the *English* Merchants , but without successe , for the King was not to
be heard of , nor seen , nor to be spoken with ; at length two Lords sent
from the King of *Denmark* , came to
Elsenore Castle , whither also the Captaines of the *English* Fleet went , who
vigorously pressed the Restitution of
their Merchant-men : But in answer to
this their Demand they were interroga-
ted ; Wherefore their Ambassadour had
not been admitted to Hearing at his being in *England* ? wherefore they came
so boldly into his Majesties Seas , and
so neer to his place of Residence , and
of his Castles, with so strong a Fleet , before they had given notice thereof three
weeks before?   But

But the *English* not standing to Can-
vasse these Demands, save onely to
procure satisfaction on their Pretenses,
pressed to have a positive Answer returned thereunto : Whereupon on the seven and twentieth of the said Moneth
they received a Letter from the King of
Denmark, telling them, That he would
preserve the said Ships for the Merchants,
as carefully as he had hitherto done, but
that he would not deliver them into their
hands. Whereupon the *English* Merchants, and the Masters and Sea-men,
seeing there was no hopes to get their
Ships released, abandoned them, and
came aboard of the Fleet, and straight-
way quitting the *Sound* made over a-
gaine towards *England*, but in the Night
of the following Day, which was the
last of the Moneth, the VVeather proved so dark, that the Admiral Ship
Commanded by Captaine *Ball*, steering too much towards the shore, run on
ground upon the Coast of that Sand, where
she was lost, onely all the Ships Company was saved, and it was ten to one
that the whole Fleet had not followed
her, she bearing the Lanthorne: she
was an excellent Frigat, called the *An-
telop*, carrying fifty brass Gunnes. But
this Losse was presently after repaired by
the

The *Antelope*
Frigate lost.

taking of about twenty *Holland* Barques, and one Convoy Man of Warre; as also one other Ship, carrying twenty Gunnes, and thus without any other Losse, or adventure, they returned into *England*, and on the fifteenth of *October*, they came to an Anchor in *Burlington* Bay, within a little while after Master *Bradshaw* was deputed in the quality of an Envoy, or Deputy towards the King of *Denmark*, to try whether the Restitution of those Merchants Vessels might not be procured in an amicable way, but this Attempt proved as bootlesse as the former; For the said Ships were not onely detained, but their Lading was carried on Shoare and Sold: Which Acts of Hostility committed against the Law of Nations and of Hospitality to innocent Persons, and against a State which had desired their Amity, by all wayes and means possible, will sooner, or later meet with their Reward and Punishment, either by the hands of those who were endamaged, or by some others, which by the sequell you will find proved so.

But to return againe to the *Hollander*, who were almost enraged at their continuall Losses of their Ships, with which all the Havens in *England* were filled, and being resolved to be revenged for so many

Sea

Sea Fights as they had lost, busied themselves in setting forth a great Fleet, and notwithstanding the rigour of the Season in the very midst of Winter, they came to Sea with a Fleet of ninety Saile, and ten Fire-ships; and on the twentieth of *December*, they appeared on the back of the *Goodwins*: the *English* Fleet under General *Blakes* Command, consisted but in two and forty Ships, ill furnished, wanting Men, and all other Necessaries: The greatest part of the best Ships having been rendred incapable of going forth to Sea; whereas there was the greatest occasion to make use of them, which happened either by the negligence, or rather by the perfideousness, and treachery, and set Malice of some, who at that time had the management of the Sea Affaires, being over jealous that the Military Persons and Men of Action, should grow too high and over-top them; although afterwards God in his own time found out these men, and caused them to give an account of these their pernitious averseness to the publicke Good of the Common-wealth, and to the private interests of the particular Members thereof. Howeu the *English*, notwithstanding the Inequality of their Forces, resolved to Launch out

and

and fight them so that on the thirtieth of *December* being a very faire day, both Fleets steering Westward, encountred each other about eleven of the Clock in the Morning, and began the Fight, the *English* having the upper hand of the Wind; of two and forty *English* Ships, not one halfe of them engaged in the fight for want of men, insomuch, that twenty, or two and twenty Ships bare the brunt of the puissant *Holland* Fleet. The *Avant guard*, and the *Victory*, two brave Frigats, having been the whole day engaged in the midst of the Enemy, firing from all sides, got off in a very good Condition: But towards the Evening, the *Garland*, carrying about forty pieces of Cannon, was boorded at once by two great Dutch Ships, which she manfully resisted, till her Decks were quite unfurnished of men, which having blowne up, and finally being over powered on all sides, was forced to yield. The *Bonaventure* being a Merchant-man, but a good Vessell going to relieve the *Garland*, was clapt aboord by a Man of Warre, and after she had severall times cleered her Decks of the Enemy, which were gotten into her, at length by the death of her Captaine, who behaved himselfe stoutly, she

she lost both Strength and Courage, and so fell into the hands of her Enemies.

Meanwhile, Generall *Blake*, who Commanded the *Triumph*, seeing this Disorder, plunged into the thickest of his Enemies to rescue the *Garland*, had his fore-Mast shot downe close by the Boord, and was Clapt on Boord by the Enemy, but having stoutly defended himselfe, and severall times beaten them off againe, he at length got cleare of them, and went off with the rest of his Fleet, onely with the losse of two Ships, which cost the Dutch deare enough, before they got them: and after the fight two *English* Merchant-men falling casually into the *Hollanders* hands, helped to make up the Friutes of this their great boasted of Victory over the *English*, which being in it selfe but a small Check, served onely to whet the Valour of the *English*, and to edge them on with the more vehemency to dissipate that Ecclipse which had so lately over Clouded their wonted Glory; Wherefore they made a very considerable Sea Equipage, and fitted out with all speed a brave Fleet of the best and gallantest Ships, as well to bring downe their Enemies Pride, who were devoid of all Moderation, after

this

this their pretended Succeſſe, as to ſtop and ſilence the Murmurings and Clamour of the People, againſt thoſe who at that time held and guided the Reines of the State; ſome of which behaved themſelves ſo untoward, that it could not be imagined, ſave that by a baſe and vile black pollicy they intended, together with the Ruine of Maratine Affaires, to bring Deſtruction upon the whole L A N D.

The

THE HISTORY
OF
OLIVER Lord Protector,
From his Cradle to his Tomb.

His Highneſs at that time being Gene-ral, was as it were ſeized with a kinde of horrour, by the very ſenſe of theſe diſorders, which could not be excuſed either by reaſon of the diſabillity of the Countrey, of any misfortunes, or ill accidents, nor by any imprudence, but were manifeſtly committed out of meer malice, through a blinde zealous ambition, His great ſoul did even re-proach him inwardly for letting the honour of his Countrey (as it were) fall to the ground; and that a Million of brave Merchants were ſuf-fered to run into perdition, by default of a diſ-creet Pilot to ſteer at the Helme, which was ſo ill guided; and although the Sea-affairs did not properly concerne him, He conceived how-ever, that in caſe during the General Shipwrack, he launched into the Main with ſome ſmall Barks to ſave the grand Veſſel and body of the State

L   which

which was perishing, he might do both a beneficial, commendable, and praise-worthy work.
He therefore believed that in Honour and Con-
science he was bound to dive more narrowly into the secret of the Affairs, and to employ the
keenness of his Sword to set an edge upon the
subtil Cabinet pens, and mend their bluntness
and dullness : so that after the most requisite
Orders for the arming and equipying of the
Fleet had been issued out, he hammered out some
others, for the better encouragement of the Sea-
men in general, as well Commanders and Soldiers , as Mariners. In reference whereunto it
was ordered,

1. That some musters should be advanced
them, to put themselves in a fit equipage to go
to Sea, and to leave a subsistence with their families during their absence.

2 That for every ship which was adjudged
good prize in the Admiralty, they should have
two pounds *per* Ton, and six pounds for every
peece of Canon, Brass, or Iron, as should be
found in the said Vessels, and the which should
be equally distributed amongst them in relation to the Offices they bear in the Ship which
had taken the said prize.

3. That they should have ten pound for every
peece of Cannon on board of such Ships as they
should sink, or destroy by firing, or otherwise.

4. That those who should enroll themselves
before the forty dayes should be expired, should
receive a moneths pay as a gratuity which
should not be put to accompt.

5. That

5. That Hospitalls should be erected at *Dover*, *Deal*, and *Sandwich*, for such sick and wounded Men as should be brought on shoar; and that a Stock should be settled for their maintenance, as also for the subsistence of such other sick and wounded men, as by reason of their Diseases and Wounds could not be brought on shoar, or should be too far from Hospitals.

Diverse other Ordinances of the like nature were also settled, which did wonderfully encourage the Sea-men and Mariners; so that toward the latter end of *February*, 1653. the *English* put forth a puissant Fleet to Sea, frighted with gallant men, who were resolved to fight it out, although at that time the *Hollanders* had made use of their best wits and stratagems, and had negotiated almost with all the Nations of *Europe*, to hinder the bringing into *England* any Pitch, Tarr, Masts, and such other necessaries for the Navigation.

This brave Fleet being in a longing desire to encounter their enemies; on the eighteenth of *February* about eight in the morning, descryed eighty *Holland* men of War conveying one hundred and fifty Merchant-men coming from *Bordeaux*, *Nantz*, *Roan*, and other parts of *France*; and just between the Isle of *Wight* and *Portland*, the foremost Frigots of the *English* Fleet, to wit, General *Blake* in the *Triumph*, followed by General *Dean*, and three or four others, began the fight; the rest of the English Fleet being towards the Coast, was not able to

A Fight between the English and the Hollander, near the Isle of Wight & Portland.

L 2

get up ; insomuch, that from eight in the morning till two in the afternoon , this small squadron of General *Blakes* was enforced to stand out the brunt of above thirty of the enemies ships, with which they incessantly fought, and demeaned themselves gallantly ; till at length about two in the afternoon, as aforesaid, half of the Fleet got up to them, and began the fight for good and all, which ceased not but with the dark night. The English lost the *Sampson*, a Ship which they had formerly taken from the Hollanders , and by reason she was quite shattered in pieces , they sunk her themselves after they had taken the men out of her ; however she cost the Hollanders dear , for she sunk the Sip which had so evilly entreated her. On the ninteenth of *February*; the English again made up towards the Enemy , and gave them Chase for a long while together , and forced some of their Ships upon the Sands where they destroyed them. The day following, the English again assaulted the Hollanders , and the fight became more obstinate then on the two dayes before; but at length the Enemies having their bellies full , began to fire out of their Sterns , and like unto the *Parthians* to make a running fight of it ; when as all their Merchant-men being not able to follow them , they became unto the English like unto so many Golden apples which stopped their pursuit of the Enemy. Towards the evening they came towards the height of *Bullen* , but the winde coming *North, North-East*, and consequently not fit to
regain

regain their own Coast, their fails and tackling being pretty well difordered, they refolved to come to an Anchor. The Englifh in this fight took about fifty Merchant-men and nine men of War, they funk feveral befides thofe the Enemies themfelves funk to fave their men; their Ships having been forely fhattered upon the Coaft of *France*; there were above two thoufand of their dead bodies found floating, and there were above fifteen hundred Prifoners brought up to *London*. General *Blake* was hurt in this encounter, having done as much as could be expected from a gallant Sea-man; and likewife feveral of his Officers and perfons of Mark, who behaved themfelves couragioufly, were both hurt and killed on this occafion. It is hard juftly to defcribe the lofs which the Hollanders fuftained in this brunt, by reafon that parties frequently endeavour to filence their difgraces, and that the Sea doth ufually better fwallow up and hide the events and effects of fuch bloody Sea-fights then the Land. The Hollander by this prodigious and vaft lofs, being touched to the quick, did fend a Letter to the Parliament, to endeavour to mediate a means to terminate thefe Differences, but the faid letter being figned onely by States of *Holland* and *Weft Freizland*, the Parliament made anfwer unto by a letter, witneffing their earneft defires to accommodate things in an amicable way, and fo to ftop the current of fo bloody a War, but the faid Negociation produced not the expected effect.

Mean

Mean time Fortune, which is as unconstant as the Sea it self, found out a way to produce the effects of her unstabillity better on this Element then on the Land; and this Goddess being thus exasperated at the constant prosperity of the English, would let them see that she had as great an advantage over their valour at Sea, as their Vallour had over her in their Land fights: Wherefore to bereave them of her Land-aids, she surprizeth them in forraign Seas, and causes them to feel one of her back-blows when they least of all expected it. Wherefore the English

The Phe-nix re-gained.

having by a stratagem recovered again the *Phenix* Frigot from the Hollanders, as she lay at an Anchor in the *Mole* of *Leagorne,* disposed themselves to a second encounter with the Hollanders in those Seas.

A second Sea-fight in the Levant between the English and the Dutch.

Captain *Badiley* with nine men of War set sail from *Porto-Longone,* to deliver and free certain Frigots Commanded by Captain *Appleton,* which were by twenty two Holland men of War cooped up in the *Mole* of *Legorne,* and had been detained in the like manner for several Moneths: the mischance was, that both these Squadrons could not come to fight the Hollanders at one and the self same time, for Captain *Appleton* and his Ships setting sail out of the said *Mole* sooner then they should have done, were immediately surrounded by the whole Holland Fleet, who being more in number, had also the advantage of the winde. The Dutch Admiral seconded by two other great Ships, fell upon the *Leopard* a smug Frigat, carrying fifty peece

of

of Cannon, who for the space of five hours together maintained a stout fight against all the said Ships, whereas being over-powred by the number of their men, she fell into the Enemies hands; and a Cannon-bullet having unhappily fired the *Bonaventure's* powder, occasioned the loss of her without Labour or Vallour to the Enemy, for she was blown up; a loss which otherwise would have cost them dear. The *Pilgrim* having sustained the brunt of four or five Holland Ships for a long while together had her Main and Mizen-Masts both shot down, and so was taken, being over-powred with numbers which she was not able to resist.

The *Levant-Merchant*, another English Frigot, maintained a long fight against a great *Holland* Ship of thirty six Guns, and being just on the brink of obtaining the Victory over her Enemy, (whom she sunk down-right a little after) was set upon anew by a fresh Ship as big as the former, with whom she fought two hours, and having lost all her men, was at length taken. The *Sampson* on the one side being assaulted by young *Van-Trump*, who commanded the Admiral of the Rere-Guard, and on the other side by a Fire-ship, was soon set on fire, and midst of the flames met with a Tomb which had some conformity to the noble heat with the which its company was animated. Thus you have a relation of the greatest misfortune which befell the *English* during the continuance of his whole War, and which was the more to be lamented, that it happened within sight of nine of their

L 4

own Ships, commanded by Captain *Badiley*, who could not with all his endeavours come up to joyn with them, but who was neverthelefs fo happy and fo prudent as to fave his fquadron, after he had done the beft to relieve his companions, and had feen that the difafter was not to be remedied.

But let us for a while quit the Sea, and take a view of fome Land paffages, and fee in what a pofture the Affairs of great *Brittain* are with the neighbouring States.

It is a thing worthy of obfervation and admiration both together, that our Protectors Anceftors did alwayes bear this Motto in their Arms, *Pax quæritur Bello* : which feemeth onely to belong to Soveraign Princes, as if by a prophetical chance, or elfe rather by a Divine Providence, this Family, which as it feems was defigned to bear the Scepter, and to reftore and give peace unto *England* after fo bloody a Civil War, and fo many other forreign broyls, had received this glorious Motto as an earneft of its future *Grandeur*; which faid Motto doth in fubftance contain all the myftery of thePoliticks, and comprehend the two powers which God doth give to thofe whom he eftablifheth his Lievetenants upon Earth. In effect, we may obferve that peace which feemed to have embraced our incomparable *Oliver*, and as it were to have been incorporated with him, hath ever fince grown up with him, until fuch time as its powerful branches, which encreafed and grew up to an infinite height, had fpread it felf fo far,

as

as that this dutiful Daughter of Heaven whose growth is limitted by God, being not able to follow him no longer, was constrained onely to fix her self to the body of the tree, and to suffer the branches to extend themselves to the other sides of the Sea-Coasts, for to deprive that Nation of Peace which doth least deserve it, having extended the War and her Tyrannies throughout all the inhabitable parts of the World. For as soon as his late Highness, our dread Protector, had attained to the power (by the means and force of Arms) in *England*, *Scotland*, and *Ireland*, Peace immediately brake forth, and resplendently shown throughout all those parts, and stopt those floods of Blood which could never have been stanched, but by the greatest branches of our illustrious *Oliver*: and not sooner had his Voice a transcendency in and over the Councels, but Peace continually accompanied his Oracles. Do but with me track the course of his fortunes, and you will finde that bright *Astrea* doth follow, or rather doth conduct and lead by the hand this blessed Deity, and chains her up to the triumphal Chariot, there to humble her and to make her know, that this our *Oliver* was not the work of her hands, but rather of her own, since it is the end which doth alwayes Crown glorious and magnanimous Actions. Now whereas the last Victory which General *Blake* obtained at Sea, had gained a great stock of credit unto his late Highness, both at home and abroad; the whole English Nation began to witness a desire

that

that he would undertake the Management of Affairs, and put himself at the Helme of the Government; and likewise all Strangers and Forreigners endeavoured to be in a good understanding with *England.* The King of *Portugal*

A *Portugal* Am-baffadour obtains Peace.

sent an extraordinary Ambaffadour over into *England,* with a gallant retinue, the ftatelinefs whereof favoured of the profufion of Peace, which was also immediately granted them on very advantageous Conditions for *England.*

And almoft at the fame time, two deputations were admitted from *France,* which Kingdom was again for the fecond time unfortunately divided by a Civil War. The French King by his Deputy demanded the reftitution of thofe Ships which had been taken by the Englifh, as they were going to the relief of *Dunkirk*; and

French Deputations fent to *England*.

on the other part, the Prince of *Conde* fent a Deputy from *Bordeaux* (befieged by the King) to demand relief; but all the Civility *England* could fhew either of them at that time, was, not to affent at all to their demands, and by that means remove all occafions of jealoufie from each party: befides that bufinefs being too much exafperated between *England* and *France,* there could not fo fuddain an occomodation be expected; and as to the *Bourdelois,* all men know thofe French Quarrels are as fhort as violent.

Deputations concerning a peace with *Holland*.

In like manner, feveral other forreign Princes and States fent over Deputations into *England,* to endeavour to moderate a Peace between this Commonwealth and the *Hollanders,* as amongft the

the rest, the Queen of *Sweeden*; The *Cantons* of *Switzer*, the Imperial Hanfiatick Towns of *Hamborough* and *Lubeck*: But at that time there was fuch a combuftion in the minde of the *Englifh*, who were at variance amongft themfelves, as that there was no appearance of thinking of any peace with ftrangers and forreigners. Affairs being therefore thus embroyled at home; his late Highnefs, as then General, feeing that in the Parliament, the particular Interefts overfwayed the publick Good, and that it was aparent, all their drifts tended but to eftablifh themfelves into a perpetual Senate, contrary to the ancient Cuftomes and Liberties of *England*, which require that Parliaments fhould have their fucceffions, and fhould onely be convocated from time to time; and that therefore the members of the houfe wiredrawed Affairs by unneceffary Centeftations, which onely ferved to publifh the defigns, and to retard the execution of them. This our General, I fay, who was defigned by the Divine Providence to eftablifh peace and tranquillity in *England* upon furer, more follid, and more glorious Foundations, entred the Parliament Houfe, accompanied by the Chief Officers of the Army, and briefly reprefented unto them the Reafons why the Parliament ought to be diffolved; which was alfo accordingly done. The Speaker with the reft of the Members immediately departing the Houfe, fome by force, fome through fear, and others not without a great deal of reluctancy and murmuring. No one living foul was aggrieved at this

The long Parliament diffolved.

this action, neither was it so much as endeavoured to be questioned or redressed by any one, all the world believing, that in case the said change should bring no good with it, at least it would not put Affairs in a worse predicament then they were : so that the sovereign Senate was dissolved, as you have heard, and the power thereof was transferred into the hands of those who better deserved it, since they acquired it by the points of their Swords; and that they have since made appear, that they knew how to use it with more prudence and moderation. Nay, the Parliament-men were even made so cheap unto the people, that they became their reproach and obliquie, and so were a consolation to the unfortunate, who saw themselves revenged on them by those from whom they had least cause to suspect or expect it. There was not so much as the least questioning nor censuring of the cause of this revolution, but every one found it expedient according unto the several satisfactions which he thereby received or hoped for; and as the Army was onely looked upon as Souldiers of fortune, whom the necessity of the Affairs, or the dangerous conjuncture of the times had enforced to take up Armes, so that which was past and gone was not laid to their charge; and the world could not choose but applaud them for what happened at present, but expect from them for the future that generosity which the Millitary profession doth inspire into great courages, as to this very day all men do enjoy, and are sensible of the favourable

able effects which have since been produced. However, the universal joy which was so evidently to be seen in all their countenances did not hinder, but that it was thought fitting for the better satisfaction of the generality, and of all men in particular, to publish the causes, the grounds and reasons of the dissolving of the Parliament, which was accordingly ordered by the General and by his Councel, consisting of the chief Officers of the Army, and was manifested accordingly in a Declaration, whereof the following are the chief Heads.

That after God was pleased marvellously to appear for his people, in reducing *Ireland* and *Scotland* to so great a degree of peace, and *England* to perfect quiet, whereby the Parliament had opportunity to give the people the harvest of all their Labour, Blood, and Treasure, and to settle a due liberty in reference to Civil and Spiritual things, whereunto they were obliged by their duty, engagements, and those great and wonderful things God had wrought for them; But they made so little progress, that it was matter of much grief to the good people of the Land, who thereupon applied themselves to the Army, expecting redress by their means; who though unwilling to meddle with the Civil Authority, agreed that such Officers as were members of Parliament, should move them to proceed vigorously in reforming what was amiss in the Common-wealth, and in settling it upon a Foundation of Justice and Righteousness; which being done, it was hoped the Parliament

The Lord General Cromwel and his Councells Manifest for the dissolving the Parliament.

liament would have answered their expectations.
But finding the contrary, they renewed their desires by an humble Petition in *August*, 1652.
which produced no considerable effect, nor was
any such progress made therein as might imploy
their real intentions to accomplish what was pe-
titioned for, but rather in averseness to the things
themselves, with much bitterness and aversion
to the people of God, and his Spirit acting in
them, insomuch that the Godly party in the Army were rendred of no other use then to countenance the ends of a corrupt party for effecting
their desires, in perpetuating themselves in the
supreme Government. For the obviating of
these evils, the Officers of the Army obtained
several meetings with some of the Parliament,
to consider what remedy might be applied to
prevent the same; but such endeavours proving
ineffectual, it became evident that the Parliament through the corruption of some, the jealousie of others, and the non-attendance of many, would never answer those ends which God,
his People, and the whole Nation expected
from them; But that this Cause which God had
so greatly blessed, must need languish under
their hands, and by degrees be lost; and the
Lives, Liberties, and Comforts of his people
be delivered into their Enemies hands: all
which being sadly and seriously considered by
the honest people of the Nation, as well as by
the Army, it seemed a duty incumbent upon us
who had seen so much of the power and presence
of God, to consider of some effectual means
where-

whereby to establish Righteousness and Peace in these Nations. And after much debate it was judged necessary, That the supreme Government should be by the Parliament devolved upon known persons, fearing God, and of approved integrity, for a time, as the most hopeful way to countenance all Gods people, reforme the Law, and administer Justice, impartially, hoping thereby the people might forget *Monarchy*, and understand their true interest in the election of successive Parliaments; that so the Goverment might be settled upon a Right *Basis*, without hazard to this glorious Cause, or necessitating to keep up Armies for the defence of the same. And being still resolved to use all means possible to avoid extraordinary courses, we prevailed with about twenty Members of Parliament to give us a Conference, with whom we plainly debated the necessity and justness of our proposals, the which found no acceptance, but instead thereof, it was offered, that the way was to continue still this Parliament, as being that from which we probably might expect all good things. This being vehemently insisted on, did much confirme us in our apprehensions, that any love to a Representative, but the making use thereof to recrute, and so to perpetuate themselves, was their aim in the Act they had then under consideration. For preventing the consumating whereof, and all the sad and evil consequences which upon the grounds aforesaid must have ensued, and whereby at one blow the interest of all honest men, and of this glorious

rious

rious cause had been endangered to be laid in the dust, and these Nations embroiled in new troubles, at a time when our Enemies abroad are watching all advantages against, and some of them actually engaged in War with us, we have been necessitated (though with much repugnancy) to put an end to this Parliament. This Declaration and these proceedings of his late Highness, then General, and of his Councel of Officers of the Army, were backed by the consent of the Generals at Sea, and by all the Captains of the Fleet, and in like manner by all the other Generals and Officers of the Land forces, both in *Stotland*, *Ireland*, and the other Territories.

But least the Magistrates and other publick Ministers of Justice and Policy, surprized at this suddain change, should chance to swerve from their duties; or that other persons should thereby take occasion to foment disturbances prejudicial to the Common-wealth, this ensuing Declaration was published. Whereas the Parliament being dissolved, persons of approved fidelity and honesty are, according to the late Declaration of the two and twentieth of *April* last past, to be called from the several parts of this Common-wealth to the supreme authority; and although effectual proceedings are, and have been had for perfecting those resolutions, yet some convenient time being required for the assembling of those persons, It hath been found necessary for preventing the mischiefs and inconveniencies which may arise in the mean while

A Declaration for settling a Councel of State.

to

to the publick Affairs, that a Council of State be conſtituted to take care of, and intend the peace, ſafety, and preſent management of the Affairs of this Common-wealth; which being ſettled accordingly, the ſame is hereby declared and publiſhed, to the end that all perſons may take notice thereof, and in their ſeveral places and ſtations, demean themſelves peaceably, giving obedience to the Laws of the Nation as heretofore, in the exerciſe and adminiſtration whereof, as endeavours ſhall be uſed. That no oppreſſion or wrong be done to the people, ſo a ſtrict accompt will be required of all ſuch as ſhall do any thing to endanger the publick peace and quiet upon any preſence whatſoever, Dated *April* the thirtieth 1653. ſubſcribed *Oliver Cromwel.*

Theſe domeſtick revolutions did in a manner put a new life into the Dutch again, who thought that they would cauſe ſome eminent diſtractions and diſturbances as well on the Seas as by Land. But they were very much deceived, for the Maratine Affairs of theſe Lands, on which either the good or bad fortune of *England* depended, were carryed on with ſo much dexterity, diligence, and vigour, as that they had reaſon to confeſs, that the change of the Pilot, and the entire obedience which is rendered to an abſolute Captain, who hath the ſole power in his hands, are but ill ſigns that the Veſſel ſhould be therefore the worſe guided and conducted. And to give you a proof of the truth, the Hollanders having at that time a vaſt number of Merchant-men in
M   their

their Harbours ready to set Sail, durst not hazard them through the Channel, although they had a Fleet of ninety Men of War to conduct them. But conducted them by North of *Scotland* to reach the Sound, where they met with another great Fleet of their Merchant-men, some coming from *Russia*, some from the *East-Indies*, and others from *France*, all which they carryed home into *Holland*; after which, hearing that the English Fleet was steered Northward, instead of seeking them out, and to take the advantage of the English divisions, as they had pretended and bragged, they amuzed themselves in making several bravadoes in such places where there was neither honour, glory, nor benefit to be acquired: at length they steered towards the Downs where they carried away two or three despicable Barks, and sent some volleys of Cannon into *Dover*, their Hearts and their Sails being equally puffed up with these imaginary successes, which savouring something of their old Masters Jack Spaniards Rodomontado's, they thought they could not better express them then at that time, saying, That the English Fleet was to be cryed out by the sound of Trumpets and Horns, as if she had been lost. But the Winde being as unconstant as the Sea it self, and as dangerous, quickly tacked about to their confusion, and the Old Proverb, *That all the evil comes from the North*, was made good to their cost and charges.

For the English Fleet returning on a suddain from the Northward, on the twenty eighth of
May

May came into *Yarmouth-Road*, and on the first of *June* next ensuing, being at an Anchor, they discovered two Dutch Galliots, to which they gave chase till they came up to the body of the Dutch Fleet. But the weather proving over-covered and dusky, they could not joyn with them. On the third, the English being at Anchor near unto the South-point of the *Gober*, descryed the Enemy about two Leagues to Leeward of them, being about one hundred Sail of Ships, wherefore without loss of time the English weighed, and made up to them. The engagement began between eleven and twelve at noon, and for some hours the fight was sharp untill about six in the evening; the enemy bare right way before the winde, and so ended that dayes fight. On the next morning both Fleets came in sight of each other, but there was so little winde stirring that they could not engage each other till twelve at noon; when as they fell to it again for good and all, and after four hours fight, which proved very disadvantagious to the Hollanders, they thought it not fitting to contest any longer, but to get away as well as they could; However a fresh westerly gale arising very opportunely, the English being encouraged by their flight, bare in so hard amongst them, that they took eleven Men of War and two water Hoyes: in which fight one thousand five hundred prisoners were taken, and six Captains, besides which, six Holland Men of War were sunk, and all the rest of the Dutch Fleet had according to all probability been cut

A Fight between the English and the Dutch on the North Foreland.

The Dutch worsted and many Ships taken.

M 2 off,

off, had not the night happily closed in for them. But the darkness growing on, and the English finding themselves near the Flats, and necessitated to stay and mend their Sails and Rigging, which were much shattered and torne, about ten at night they came to an Anchor. The greatest loss the English sustained was of General *Dean* one of their Admirals, who was taken off by a great shot in the first dayes ingagement, and whose death did sufficiently recompence all the Enemies loss; he having been a person of reputed Valour and great experience, besides which, there was one Captain slain, and about one hundred and fifty men, and two hundred and forty hurt, but not one of the English Ships were lost. That which greatly encouraged the English and disheartned the Dutch, was the arival of General *Blake* to their aid and succour with sixteen good Men of War very opportunely. Now the Dutch by the favour of the night being gotten off, and having retired themselves into the *Weilings*, the , and the *Texel*, the English called a Councel of all the Officers, to advise on, what would be most expedient to be undertaken to improve this Victorie to the best advantage; and it was resolved, to advance with the whole Fleet as fast as they could to the *Weilings* as far as they could possibly approach with safety, by reason of the Flats and Shelves, and in this wise forrage the whole Dutch Coasts till they came to *Texel*: which being accordingly performed, and being arrived at the said height, they there remained a pretty while, taking every day some prizes more or less, to the great prejudice

of

of the Dutch, whose Ships could neither get in The Hollanders
pursued
and block-
ed up in
their own
Ports. or out of any of their Ports, as long as the English continued there : Nor could their Men of
War unite and come to a head to make a body
to come forth. Wherefore leaving them to take
breath, and to recollect their spirits again , and
so to think of the best means for their Deliverance, we will return for *England* again with
our Fleet and see how squares stands there.

General *Cromwel* who alwayes made use of
more moderation then power in the Rise of his
Fortune, being unwilling to deprive *England* of
her ancient Liberties and Priviledges , resolved
together with the chief Officers of his Army to
assemble a Parliament. To invest them with the
power of administring and exercising the Laws,
and to appoint them as it were Judges of his
Councel and Government. And the Warrants
requisite thereunto were issued out unto such
persons as through *England, Scotland,* and *Ireland*, were chosen by himself and his Councel,
to assist in the said Parliament , for them to
meet in the Councel-Room at *white-Hall* on
the fourth day of the moneth of *July*, in the year
of our Lord. 1653. A forme of which said War-
rant you have, as followeth, *viz.*

*Forasmuch as upon the dissolution of the late
Parliament, it became necessary that the Peace,
Safety, and good Government of this Commonwealth
should be provided for ; and in Order thereunto; diverse persons fearing God, and of approved fidelity
and honesty, are by my self, with the advice of my
Councel of Officers, nominated, to whom the great*
charge

charge and trust of so weighty Affairs is to be Committed. And having good assurance of the love to, and courage for God, and the interest of his Cause, and the good people of this Commonwealth, I Oliver Cromwel, *Captain General, and Commander in chief of all the Army and Forces raised and to be raised within this Commonwealth, do hereby Summon and Require you (being of the persons nominated) personally to be and appear at the Councel-Chamber, commonly called or known by the name of the Councel-Chamber at* White-Hall, *within the City of* Westminster *upon the fourth day of* July *next ensuing the date hereof; then and there to take upon you the said trust to which you are hereby called and appointed to serve as a member for the County of   , and hereof you are not to fail. Given under my hand and seal the   day of* July, 1653. *subscribed* Oliver Cromwel.

And in conformity to this Convocation, the nominated for every County did accordingly meet on the fourth of *July* in the Councel Chamber, where the Lord General *Cromwel,* being accompanied with the greatest part of the Officers of the Army, delivered himself to the said members in an excellent Speech; in which, his Prudence, Valour, and Piety, were at once manifested; but chiefly his passionate tenderness for the good of the Commonwealth in General, and for the peace and tranquillity of each member in particular : so that we may justly attribute unto him the qualities both of a *Cesar,* and of a *Moses,* by reason of his elegant Speech which he prosecuted in this manner.

By

By reeounting the many wonderful Mercies of God towards this Nation, and the continued Series of Providence by which he had appeared, in carrying on his Cause, and bringing Affairs to that present glorious condition wherein they were. He likewife manifefted the progrefs of Affairs fince the famous Victory at *Worcefter*, as alfo the actings of the Army thereupon: After divers applications to the Parliament, and much waiting upon them, with the Grounds and neceffities of their diffolving the laft Parliament, which he declared to be for the prefervation of this Caufe, and the Intereft of all honeft men who had been engaged therein.

In like manner, he fet forth the clearnefs of the Call given to the Members then prefent, to take upon them the Supreme Authority; and from the Scriptures exhorted them to their duties, and encouraged them therein. He further defired them, that a tendernefs might be ufed towards all confcientious perfons of what Judgement foever. Which faid Speech was pronounced with fuch a grate tone, and in fuch excellent manner, as it fufficiently manifefted, that as he himfelf was throughly perfwaded thereof, the Spirit of God acted in and by him, he had adorned it with no other eloquent phrafe, fave that of Holy Writ. The reft was a mafculine and convincing ftile, the comelinefs whereof confifted in its plainnefs, without any Rhethorical or Artificial words, but fingle and pure, fuch as proceeded from our Saviours Minifters, the

M 4   which

which begat the peace, tranquillity, and glory
of all men.

The In-
ftrument
of Go-
vernment
delivered
to the Par-
liament.
The Lord Generals Speech being ended, he
produced an Inftrument under his own Hand
and Seal, whereby he did with the Advice of his
Officers, devolve and intruft the Supreme Authority and Government of this Common-
wealth into the Hands of the perfons there met
in the manner aforefaid; who, or any Forty of
them, were to be held and acknowledged the
Supreme Authority of this Nation : unto whom,
all perfons within the fame, and the Territories
thereunto belonging, were to yield obedience
and fubjection. That they were to fit no longer
then the third of *November*, 1654. And that
three moneths before their diffolution, they
were to make choice of other perfons to fucceed
them, and whofe Powers and Sitting fhould not
exceed twelve Moneths time; at the end of
which, they were likewife to take care for a fuc-
ceffion in the Government. Which faid Inftrument having been thus delivered unto them
by the Lord General, he did again exhort them
to take the Bufinefs to heart, and to fet nothing
before their eyes fave the Glory of God, and
the Good of Publick Weal; promifing them,
that on his part, he would neither fpare his
Goods, Life, nor his Reft, to anfwer that great
Mercy of God which he had fhown them, in
making choice of them to follow thofe tracks
which the Divine Providence had fet before
them for their good, and for the glory and tranquility

quility of thefe Nations. Finally, he recommended them to the Almighties protection, and fo together with his Officers withdrew, leaving them to take their places in the former Parliament Houfe, and to act accordingly; who forthwith named their Speaker, and took their places, meeting in the Houfe and fitting in due form.

Upon this change of Government, *John Lilburne*, the chief of the Levellers, of whom mention was formerly made, and who had been banifhed the Land upon an Act of the foregoing Parliament, thought to be protected by this, and caft himfelf upon the Lord General; who being unwilling to interpofe matters of that nature, left him to the Law, whence he alwayes freed himfelf by a moft ftrong fatality of Fortune.

John Lilburn demands Protection is denied and remitted to the Law.

And whileft this new Parliament is fettling it felf in *England*, let us look a while back into *Scotland* and *Ireland*, and fee how things have profpered there fince we left them. Now although the Englifh were poffeffed of the beft ftrong places and Forterefles of all *Scotland*, and of all the Caftles and Forts of value in the Low-lands, yet however the High-landers who perceived their inacceffible Fortreffes, did make continual excurfions on the Low-lands, being a people hardy and laborious, faring hardly, ufed to the cold and rigoroufnefs of thofe Climates, as fwift and nimble as Stags; and however they have more Valour then Conduct, and more Temerity then Difcipline, yet fome of them chofe
to

The ftate of Affairs in Scotland.

to be commanded by *Glencarne*, *Athol*, the Lord *Seafort*, and others; who framing several small Bodies of them, would unexpectedly fall in upon, and surprize the Inhabitants and English Souldiery, without either giving or taking quarter, spoiling and murthering all that came in their way; and when the English would make shew to charge them, and to pursue them, in case they found themselves to be the weaker, they then betook themselves to their heels with such swiftness, and sheltering themselves in such unaccessible Rocks and Holds, that it was impossible to pursue or light upon them: by which advantages they were emboldned to commit several outrages, murthers; and had like to have surprized an English Ship which came to an anchor at *Leevis* Island, some of which ships company going on shore to get in fresh water and provisions, were detained by the Lord *Seafort*, who also sent a ridiculous Summons to the said ship for its surrender, freighted with threats and detestations of the English Government, although the said ship the *Fortune*, bearing more sails then their threats could fill, laughed at their temerity, and got off at will.

The state of Affairs in *Ireland*. Moreover, the state of Affairs in *Ireland* were much about the same predicament; for the English having reduced all the strong Holds of that Countrey, and having shipt away all those who had born Arms in the last Wars, to be transported into *Spain*, *France*, *Flanders*, and other parts whither themselves would go, those onely excepted, who during the first Rebellion, had a hand

hand in the murthering of the Proteſtants, and who were brought up through all the parts of the Countrey, were tryed, condemned, and exscuted in great numbers, they drave the reſt of the Iriſh into *Cannaught*, within the heart or center of the Countrey; where they are coopsed in by the Engliſh, who have poſſeſſed their Lands, and have given them others in that Province to the value of them: however, the Engliſh were continually moleſted by the Out-laws of that Nation, the *Tories*, much like the *Moſs-Troopers*, or Italian *Bandittoes*, but of late they are pretty well calmed, and almoſt quite exterminated.

Mean while the continual Wars in *Ireland*, as well as the ſaid Baniſhment and Executions, having left above one half of *Ireland* almoſt as it were deſart, and left all the reſt of the Coutrey as a prey to the Conquerour; hereupon his late Highneſs made uſe of this occaſion to give an evidence both of his Juſtice and Prudence together. For whether the Exchequer at that time was bare of Moneys or no, or whether this great Politician had wilfully deferred the paying of the Engliſh Forces in *Ireland* till this very time, the better to ſettle the Engliſh in thoſe parts, he gave unto them thoſe Lands which themſelves had conquered, in part of their payment; whereby he did according to the uſual ſaying, kill two birds with one ſtone, if not three; which is, that at the ſame alſo he did recompenſe them with that which was far more worth then that which was owing unto them, and a far

An admirable effect of his Highneſs Prudence and Juſtice

more

more worth then that, which was owing unto them, and a far more folid thing, which was not to be eafily taken from them ; fo that part of the Irifh Lands were alotted to pay the Souldiery, and at the fame time to eftablifh and fettle the Conquefts of *Ireland*, by giving them a fubfiftence to maintain and preferve them in thofe parts. As for the other part of the faid Lands, we muft look back, how in the beginning of thefe Wars, the State being not in a capacity to furnifh fufficient monies to defray the charges thereof, was Conftrained to borrow monyes of private perfons on the promifes of paying them both Principal and Intereft, as foon as the Conquefts of *Ireland* fhould be perfected ; and however fince that time the fcene of Affairs was mightily changed, that thofe who were engaged in this promife, and who at that time governed the State, had no more power or might , and that his late Highnefs was not in reafon bound to fubfcribe or make good thofe Conditions or Articles on which they received the faid *monies*, nor to heed the fame at all ; yet however by a tranfcendent act of Juftice he confented unto the difpofal of the remaining Lands towards the reinburfing of the Irifh Adventurers, and by this means made his Laurels become as fruitful as if they had been watred by the fweat and labours of thofe people, and brought up at their cofts and charges ; fo that he both fatisfied the Souldiers Arrears, and the Adventurers Advances to their own content and hearts defires, and to his own praife and glory as long as the memory of man lafteth.

Mean

Mean while the Hollanders being quite tired by their continual losses, and seeing that Fortune remained obstinate to their prejudice, and seldome or never frowned on the English, resolved at length once more to come to a Treaty, and to this purpose sent four Commissioners into *England*, viz. the Lords, *Beveringe, Newport, Yongstal*, and *Vanderperre*, which last no sooner arived here, but took leave of the world; so that the other three pursued their Negotiation with hopes of a good success: yet however these fair appearances did not produce either a cessation or a suspension of Armes, but both parties treated and fought together, insomuch that all kinde of hostilies were exercised on both sides against each other; and as they seemed both desirous to shew the most of their powers, and that there was no necessity at all of a peace, so they came at length to a notable fight even during the Treaty, and the which did not a little conduce to hasten the Conclusion of the peace. The manner of which fight was as followeth.

On the twenty ninth of *July*, two English Scouts, where abroad at Sea on intelligence, discovered the Holland Fleet coming forth of the *Wielings* of about ninety five sail, all men of War; and as soon as the English Fleet received notice thereof, they made all the sail they possibly could toward them, but the Enemies discrying our Fleet, witnessed a desire not as yet to fight and so stood away. But by five of the clock that evening some of the English Frigots getting up

[margin notes:] Continuance of the Dutch Affairs.

Holland Commissioners sent over to treat.

A notable fight between the Dutch and English during the Treaty.

up to them, engaged them into a Fight; and
soon after, thirty of our Ships seconding of
them, began the Fight for good and all, and
were constrained to bear the brunt of the whole
Holland Fleet, by reason the rest of the English
Fleet being asterne could not get up to engage.
However they were onely separated by the night
which forced both Fleets to retreat; and the
Fight although it was but short, yet it proved
smart, and the Hollanders had several of their
Ships put out of a condition to serve, being so
soarly maimed, that they were forced to send
them away in the night, by the favour whereof
they got by the English, and strove to joyn
with a relief of five and twenty good Ships which
which were coming to the mouth of the *Texel.*

The Fight
renewed.
On the morrow, the Hollanders being encouraged by their new recruits which they had
joyned with the night before, by reason of the
thick and sowl weather which hindred the English from debarring them thereof, fell first of
all upon the English Fleet with a great deal of
gallantry and resolution; and from five in the
morning till one in the afternoon fought as cou-
ragiously as possibly men could, either in respect of the Valour they shewed, or in their
conduct and dexterity in mannaging of the said
Fight; and the English on their sides being well
pleased to have to do with so gallant and resolute an enemy, and who promised them a great
deal of glory in their manful and vigorous resistance, received them as gallantly on their
parts; and the fight being by this time well exasperated

asperated on both sides, they passed through, and upon each other with so much violence, impetuosity, and dexterity, as that it might be easily conjectured each particular person knew that the whole decision of the War depended on the event of this combat. The Sea was never so much pressed by its contrary Elements, and the combatants which covered the Decks and Galleries appeared like unto so many Salamanders that live in the fire; and indeed the zeal and earnestness which transported them were of the very same nature; each Vessel chose another to try the day withal, and whensoever one was charged by two or three, more or less, that onely served to waken her dexterity, and to excite her resolution; And those who could not burn, destroy, or sink their Enemies by a close boarding and grasping hand to hand, endeavoured to dispute that which their Cannons could not effect. The Fight at length became so obstinate and violent, as that the Air was red by fire, and the Sea with blood, and these two floating Forests, whose high and thick Masts sunk as fast as the Corn under the Mowers hand, gave to believe by their redoubled and obstinately continued blows, that the Sea would at length serve both the Fleets for a *Triumph* and a Tomb.

And in the very midst of this contest, the Holland Admiral *Van-Trump* being wounded, presaged his death, wherefore like a Lion, who having received his mortal wound by the hand of the Huntsman, redoubleth his force ever at the Article of his expiring; so this famous and renowned

The Dutch Admiral *Van-Trump* slain.

nowned Admiral did sell his life at a dear rate,
and had received that happiness to be sprinkled
with the blood of his Enemies in that barbarous
Element in which he had so often sown his
Palms and Laurels.

In like manner, the Generals *Blake* and *Monk*
did most admirably well sustain the last Assaults
of this desperate dying Admiral, who desired
not so much to live as to revenge his own
Death. Both these gallant Generals I say were
present every where, and in all occasions; and
where their persons could not shew themselves,
Vice-Admiral *Pen* and Rere-Admiral *Lawson*, so
well supplied their places, as that the Hollanders encountred none but Admirals wheresoe-
ever they charged. Finally, all the English as
well Officers as Sea-men behaved themselves
wonderously well, and had the Honour to obtain joyntly with the Laurels of War, the Ro-
ses and Olive-branches of a glorious Peace. And
amongst the rest of the Holland Ships of note,
the *Garland* a stout man of War, which the Hollanders had formerly taken from the English
was laid aboard by the *Worcester* Frigot, and
was fired and burnt by her. The *Triumph* and
the *Andrew* of the English side were also boarded by two or three Dutch Fire Ships, and received some dammage in their sails and rigging, but
were quickly again cleared by the Valour and industry of the nearest Ships, and some of particular persons. As to the Hollands Fleet, it seemed
to have been all on fire, so well did the English
Fire Ships second by their dexterity the men of
War,

War, and the Cries of those who saw their ships rouling and sinking alike, were more formidable and loud then the roarings of the Sea; so that as they endeavoured to avoid the flames, they were sure to finde their deaths, in the mercilesse Waves. There were at least twenty Holland men of War burnt and sunk in this fight, and almost all their Companies lost; although the English took more glory to save them, then their valour as it seems had to destroy them, the generosity of the English causing them to precipitate themselves midst all dangers whatsoever, to save the lives of above a thousand of their enemies: amongst which, there were six Captains which the Hollanders themselves had abandoned, by reason they were not in a capacity to save them.

o Finally, the Hollanders seeing so great a number of their ships sunk and lost, began to despair of the Victory; and the spirits of their men being drowned and fallen, they thought it not fitting to expose themselves with the rest of the Fleet, to the hazard of a general defeat and rout, they faced about, and began to bear away with all the possible sail they could make towards the *Texel.* And the English not judging it expedient to engage too far upon the Dutch Coast by reason of the Flats, the Winde being also very uncertain and inconstant at that time, and moreover their sails and tackling being sufficiently tora and rent, they resolved at a Councel of War, to set sail with the whole Fleet to *Soles-Bay*, to dispose of such ships as were disabled

The Dutch put to flight.

N

abled, and to put their wounded Men and Prisoners on shore, and sending two small Frigots
to observe the Course they steered, who kept in
sight of them till next morning by break of day,
when as they steered into *Texel* Harbor, by the
favour of certain Boats with Lights, which were
sent them out to conduct them in. The loss
which the English sustained in this Fight, was
of about three hundred men who were slain
out-right; amongst which there were eight
Captains, to wit, *Graves, Chapman, Taylor,
Newman, Crispe, Owen, Cox,* and *Peacock*; the
wounded were about seven hundred in number,
whereof five were Captains, *viz. Stokes, Sea-
man, Rous, Holland,* and *Cubitt,* who all of them
behaved themselves like persons of Courage and
Conduct. As for the number of the *killed and
hurt* on the Hollanders part, we can make no
other guess thereat, save onely according to the
number of the ships which they lost, however
several Letters from *Holland* certified, that in the
Fight they lost about six thousand men.

This Naval Conflict being the most bloody
and most famous Fight which happened between
the English and the Hollander since the Wars
began, did evidently manifest what a kinde of
Martial genious it was, that had gotten such a
transcendency upon the deciding of a Victory;
and how wise and vigorous a Pilot there was
both at the Helm of the State and of the Fleet:
So likewise the advantages which were obtained
by this Victory were very considerable, during
the conjuncture of Affairs at the present, just on
the

the point of an accomodation, which also enfu-
ed both unto the profit, honour, and glory of
England. And in reference thereunto, the Parliament did acknowledge this so important and
confiderable a peace of fervice by all the marks
of honour, which could be worthily conferred
on perfons who had so valiantly acquitted
themfelves. To the Generals, *Blake, Monk,
Pen,* and *Lawfon,* and to the other Flag Captains, Gold Chains were prefented as precious
tokens of their favour and acknowledgements;
and to the other Officers of the Fleet, filver Med-
dals were diftributed, which although they were
not of so much value yet they bear as great
a weight in the Scales and Ballances of honour
and glory.

And this very Parliament which truly had
procured very beneficial Orders in matters of
the leffer confequence, extreamly advantagious
to the people, in refpect of the fmall time during
which they had been affembled, however in the
greater concernments they had not so good Fortune; there was so much of confufion in their
Councels, fuch a contrariety in their opinions,
fuch a diffonancy in their actings, and difparity
in their aims and projections, as that this Senate
was more like unto a Monfter with many heads,
then a well ordered grand affembly, or fupreme
Councel; infomuch, that there was little or
no appearance it should continue out the prefixed time of their fitting. Moreover, the chief-
eft defignes by their long and tedious difcuffions
and debates did even perish and vanish through

The weakneß of the new Parliament.

the

the loſs of thoſe urgent actions which are the ſoul of execution, or became publick by a too publick devulging of ſuch ſecrets as are not uſually diſcovered by great Stateſmen, untill the very effects of them are ready to appear. All which reaſons being naturally pondered by the wiſeſt and moſt zealous perſons intereſſed in the glory of the Engliſh Nation, the good and wellfare of the Commonwealth, and particularly by his excellency the Lord General, it was reſolved that the Parliament ſhould be diſſolved ; in reference hereunto, on the twelfth of *December*, 1653. as ſoon as the Parliament was met, A Member of the ſaid Houſe ſtood up and moved.

A motion to diſſolve the Parliament.

That the ſitting of this Parliament as it was then conſtituted, being not thought proper nor fitting for the good of the Commonwealth, It was therefore requiſite to deliver up unto the Lord General *Cromwel*, the powers which they had received from him. Which motion being ſeconded by the greateſt part of the other Members, the Houſe aroſe, and the Speaker accompanied by the major part of the Houſe departed, and went to *White-Hall*, where they did by a Writing under their hands (being the greater number of the Members ſitting in Parliament) reſign unto his Excellency the Power which they had received from him, and the which was by the Speaker preſented to his ſaid Excellency accordingly, in the Name of the whole Houſe.

The Parliament diſſolved *December*, 12, 1653.

No ſooner was the Parliament diſſolved and that Affairs of moment and weight came crowding in apace, but that there was a neceſſity (during
ring

ring the intervalls of Parliament) to form (as it is called in forreign parts) an upper Councel, and to create a superiour dignity, to avoid both tediousness and confusion in the dispatch of Affairs; which said dignity holding the mid-way between a Monarchial and Democratical, might avoid the inconveniencies which these two extremities are subject unto; and the thing it self having been well pondered and maturely deliberated, the choice of the person on whom this dignity was to be conferred, was soon made, God having pointed him out unto them by a mark, those admirable and uninterrupted Victories which he caused him to gain; and by those excellent productions of a minde, which had something of supernatural in it, and partaked of the Divinity.

Wherefore the Lord General *Cromwel* was Elected, Declared, and Sworn at *Westminster*, in the presence of all the Judges and Justices, the Barons of the Exchequer, the keepers of the Liberties of *England*, the Lord Major and Aldermen of the City of *London*, with most of the chief Officers of the Army, *Lord Protector* of the Commonwealth of *England*, *Scotland*, and *Ireland*; and the Islands and Territories thereunto belonging; and at the same time several Articles were presented to the Lord Protector, by which he was to govern the people; which being red unto him, he took a solemn Oath to performe and see them kept in the presence of the whole assembly, protesting moreover, that he would minde nothing so much as the

(margin note:) The Lord General *Cromwel* chosen and sworn Lord Protector.

the good of the Commonwealth; the Glory of God, and the Honour of the English Nation.

The chief heads of the Articles of Government were as followeth.

The Protector Sworn to the ensuing Articles.

1. That the Protector should call a Parliament every three years.

2. That the first Parliament should assemble on the third of *September*, 1654.

3. That he should not dissolve the Parliament till it had sate five moneths.

4. That such Bills as he should not signe within twenty dayes should pass without him.

5. That he should have a select Councel to assist him, not exceeding one and twenty, nor less then thirteen.

6. That immediately after his Death the Councel should choose another Protector before they rose.

7. That no Protector after him should be General of the Army.

8. That the Protector should have Power to make Peace or War.

9. That with the consent of his Councel he may make Laws which shall be binding to the Subjects during the intervals of Parliament, &c.

Immediately after which, the Lord General *Cromwel*, without the devesting of himself of the Command of the Army, (which he preferred before all other charges) took upon him the title of *Highness*, and the dignity and name of *Lord Protector*. A very fit appellation, in regard

gard of the Infantine, and as yet growing State of *England*, which the several Factions and Divisions, as also the different Opinions in Religion would have exposed to a numberless kinde of unavoidable miseries, had not a powerful *Genius*, armed with Force and Judgement, protected it from ripping up its Entrails and Bowels by its own hands. And immediately after, he was proclaimed *Lord Protector of England, Scotland, and Ireland,* &c. First in the Pallace-yard at *Westminster*, by the Officers of State, and afterwards at the Royal Exchange by the Lord Major and Aldermen in their Scarlet Gowns.

The Lord Protector proclaimed.

Some few dayes after the body of the City invited his Highness the Lord Protector to a most splendid feast and gallant entertainment, at *Grocers-Hall*, not so much to treat him with their good chear, as with the resplendent testimonies of their joy, and with the submissive tenders of their devoires.

His Highness would by no means refuse to give that satisfaction to their evidences of respect and joy, and the better to testifie unto them on his behalf, the high value he put upon their care and love, he set forth towards them in as great a pomp and magnificence as befitted a person invested with so eminent qualities, and as one who having reaped so many Laurels, had newly restored peace and tranquillity unto three distracted Kingdomes.

N 4   *The*

The manner of his Highness going to the City and
reception there, was on this wise.

His Highness Life-guard of Horse marched in the first place, after which followed the chief Officers of the Army on Horse-back, and some of his Councel of State; after them rode two Pages bare-headed in sumptuous Apparel; after them came twelve Lackeys in velvet Caps and gray Liveries, with silk and silver Fringe; then followed his Highness seated in a Charet of State drawn by six beautiful Horses richly trapped, which by their lofty gate seemed to glory in their drawing so victorious a *Hercules*, triumphing over so many Monsters: and his Highness who always preferred the little ornaments of the Soul before those of the Body, was onely clad in a dark coloured Suit and Cloak, the greatest part of the other Nobility attending in their Coaches and six horses.

At *Temple-Bar* his Highness was met and received by the Lord Major and Aldermen, and the Recorder of the City saluted him with an excellent Speech, containing several expressions of Joy, Fidelity, and Obeisance, and of good Hopes of his prosperous and happy Government. His Highness having thanked him, alighted from his Chariot, and quitting his Cloak, put on a rich Riding Coat imbroidered with Gold, and got up on Horse-back on a Palfrey richly trapped, and was followed by three other led Horses of State. By which change of Garments, his High-

Highness testified unto them, that when as occasions of the States-service should call upon him,
he would descend from his Triumphal Chariot,
where the glory of his Conquests had set him in
rest, and mounting his Horse for Battel; would
expose his Life as freely, as he formerly had
done, for the peace and tranquility of their City, and for the Liberty of *England*. The Lord
Major rode all the way bare-headed, as also carried the City Sword drawn before his late Highness the Lord Protector. By the one, representing the Respect and Obedience of the City; and
by the other, its Fidelity and Resolution, to spill
their Blood in the defence of the peace of the
State; and for the preservation of the Life and
new Dignity of his Highness.

The Streets were railed up, and the several
Companies of the City in their Liveries sate on
both sides of the way, with Streamers sticking
up to distinguish each Company. Moreover, it
is a thing worthy to be observed, how that the
Character which God doth imprint on the Forehead of those whom he hath designed to be his
Vicegerents on Earth, doth beget an astonishment and fear in the hearts of those where it
cannot raise a respect; but in the others, both
admiration and love: so that on all sides the Divine Providence compasseth its Glory, either by
the means of its Justice or Mercy. And thus
you see his Highness the Lord Protector passing
through this great City, which was drawn up in
Arms, having his Head onely covered with Laurels, and his guarded with a simple though resplendent

splendent morsel of Glory; The one surrounding him to cover and protect him with her wings; and the disarmed Justice which accompanied this great Heroes footsteps, seemed to Lead a naked and fettered *Mars* by a silken thread.

And thus after his Highness had been most splendedly entertained by the City, before he departed, he conferred the Honour of Knighthood upon the Lord Major, and left all the City filled with an admiration of his Heroick Vertue, and with a general satisfaction of his candor and generousness, their hopes being freighted with acclamations and good wishes.

No sooner was his late Highness settled in the Supreme degree of his Protectorship, but just like the Sun elevated in a high sublime Sphere, he begat an infinite number of malignant Exhalations, which however were soon dissipated by his luster and resplendency; and at the same time by his vertue, he gave a life and being to all those glorious actions which knowing men did expect from his sage Government.

On the Eighteenth of *February* 1653, a most dangerous Conspiracy which was hatched by the Royalists was discovered; several of the Conspirators were taken and sent to the Tower of *London*. But his Highness willing to begin his Government by an Act of Clemency, and to let the world see, that the Grandor of his new Dignity did onely render him powerful to do good, he pardoned the said Delinquents, and caused them to be set at liberty.

Much

Marginal notes:
Sir *Thomas Viner* Knighted.

A Conspiracy discovered.

Much about which time arrived Deputies Addresses to his Highness from all parts. from the several Counties and Shires as well of *England, Scotland* and *Ireland*, to congratulate his Highness happy Inauguration, and to assure him of their fidelity and submission to his Commands; all which his Highness received with a great deal of Candor, and repaied them with Use (to wit) the establishing of good and salutary Orders for the Peace and Tranquility of the Commonwealth, and each Member thereof in particular; Nor did he forget to regulate the Spiritual Affairs, and out of an infinite number of Opinions, he begat a pleasant harmony; the seeming dissonance and harshness whereof, was onely unsavory to the ignorant, and to such as had stopped their ears.

Mean while the Scots animated by several discontented persons here in *England*, did levy an Army by Command from their King, and began The Scots frame an Army. to take heart of grace again, reassuming their former courage and hopes. The Earls of *Glencarne* and *Kenmore* were at the Head of four thousand Horse and Foot, joyning several other small parties, which from all sides flocked down unto them. But Collonel *Morgan* was so vigilant and active, that before they could have time to Form a greater Body, he marched with fifteen hundred Horse and Foot, and on the seventh of *February* he arrived at *Lough*, which was the Enemies appointed Rendezvouz, where The Scots defeated by Collonel *Morgan*. having charged them, after a short but smart Fight, he killed one hundred and fifty of them, and defeated all the rest; the Earl of *Glencarne*

with

with much ado making his escape onely with forty Horse. But all these small Bickerings, and as it were shadows of War, did onely serve as a foil to that most important and considerable Peace which both *England* and *Holland* was to reap at our *Oliver's* hands.

When as most part of the Winter was well nigh passed over in this Negociation at *London*, where the Hollanders had four Ambassadours who daily laboured to compass the same. Two of them, to wit, the Lords *Newport* and *Youngstall* re-passed into *Holland* about the Moneth of *February*, to communicate unto the High and Mighty Lords the States their Masters, the Conclusion of the Treaty, and to get them to ratifie the same. On the third of *March* 165¾. of the same Year, they returned back again, where they were received with all the pomp and state that could possibly be imagined, and might demonstrate the Joy which the Merchants conceived of the happy effects of so happy a Reconciliation. The next day they had Audience from his Highness, where declaring the full powers they had from the Lords States to ratifie the said Peace which they had made, they desired a speedy Cessation of Arms should be published on both sides; and in conformity thereto, on the fifth Day of *April* next ensuing, the Articles of Peace were signed, sealed, and delivered on the behalf of both parties, and were accordingly published and proclaimed, to the general satisfaction of all men. And his Highness, the better to testifie the particular pleasure he took

therein,

therein, did most sumptuously treat the *Holland* Ambassadours; witnessing unto them by his noble Noble treatment, all the marks of Joy which might manifest and make good, by his Conduct and Entertainment, the old Motto of his Family, *That War hath no other end save to beget a Peace.*

And as to the Affairs of *Ireland,* his Highness by his good Orders, and establishing the Natives in the Province of *Camaught,* which is in the heart of *Ireland,* had settled all things so well in those parts, as that the English needed not to fear any either abroad or at home; and the Irish beginning to be sensible that the Yoke of a vigilant and absolute Protector was far more tollerable, and to be preferred before the Servitude of a feeble and tottering multitude, who onely heeding their own preservations and particular interests, do abandon the People and their wellfares, either to their own capriciousness, or to the imbroils of ambitious and hot spirits, who abusing of the Commonaltics simplicity and sincerity, run them headlong into Ruine.

The Affairs of *Ireland* settled.

But some enemies of the State perceiving that it was impossible to hinder the Earth from bringing forth of good fruits, as long as it was animated by so sensible and feeling a warmth, resolved to beget an Eclipse of its Sun; and having covered it with darkness, to bring down Horrour and Confusion upon it: wherefore a black Conspiracy was hatch'd again his late Highness's Life; but Heaven which had pre-served

A second conspiracy.

served him for her glory, and for the good of *England*, and carried him through so many dangers during the Wars, did even as yet watch over him in the times of Peace, and miraculously preserved him for this hainous attempt, as well as from many others. Several of the Conspirators were apprehended; and amongst the rest ,Mr. *Thomas* and *John Gerrard* , Brothers, *John Jones* an Apothecary, and *Thomas Tender*, *Somerset Fox*, and *Peter Vowel*, who being Tried and Condemned to dye, *Vowel* was Hanged, *John Gerrard* by reason of his Birth was Beheaded; *Thomas Gerrard* and *Fox* were pardoned by his Highness, by reason of their ingenuous confessions, and some other further discoveries which they made of the Fact.

Mr. *Vowel* Hanged Mr. *Gerrard* Beheaded.

At the same time the *Portugal* Ambassadors Brother was likewise Beheaded, for having caused the Death of an English Gentleman, at a hubbub and quarrel made by the *Portugals* in the New Exchange : neither could States policy , nor the complacency and gallantry which are often used by Princes, to the prejudice of the Commonwealth , and of the particular members of the same, hinder the doing of Justice in this case ; so much did the love of his Countrey, and the suffering of Justice to take place, prevail with his late Highness.

The *Portugal* Ambassadors Brother Beheaded.

Mean while, the Scotch Highlanders not being able to brook the English yoke , although they full well saw that their continual Conspiracies and Risings were discovered and crushed, yet they believed that a far greater and more con-

The Scotch Highlanders rise in Armes.

considerable one might happily break forth, and
show themselves, in case any considerable party
should rise in Armes, they therefore got together in a body; and General *Middleton* being
passed out of *Holland* into *Scotland*, joyned himself to them. But General *Monk* falling into the
North of *Scotland*, and for some time driving
them from place to place, did at length on the
one and twentieth of *July* 1654. give them such
a full charge at *Loughberrie*, that he defeated
them, and made them incapable of ever after
thinking of appearing in Armes again. However, all these happy successes, such an absolute
power, and so invincible an Army at command,
did not at all infulo in his Highnesses thoughts,
nor puff up his minde, nor inhaunced his authority, save onely armed him with much precaution as he stood in need of, to maintain the Peace
and Tranquillity of the People, to augment
their wealth, and to encrease the glory of the
Commonwealth, therefore to produce that
mediocrity which the Gown adds to Armes, and
which publick Councels do unto private Deliberations, on the third of *September* 1654. a
Parliament (which had been convocated by his
Highnes Writs according to the tenor of the
precedent ones) assembled at *Westminster*, and
began its sitting, after the members had been
present at a most learned and eloquent Sermon
preached by Mr. *Marshal*, when as Mr. *Lenthal*
was declared Speaker of the House; and as soon
as they were met, they fell upon the questioning
of the Power by which they were convocated,
and

General Middleton defeated by General Monk.

A Parliament assembly September 3. 1654.

and doubted of its lawfulnefs, fo that His late Highnefs, confidering with himfelf the evils which a new change might produce, caufed a forme and acknowledgement of the Government to be drawn up, which was to be figned by all the Members of the Houfe before they were to meet again. The Tenour whereof followeth, viz.

The Recognition to be figned by the Members before they were admitted to the Houfe in the Parliament of *September* 3. 1654.

I do hereby freely promife and engage to be true and faithful to the Lord Protector, and the Commonwealth of England, Scotland, *and* Ireland, *and fhall not (according to the Tenor of the Indenture, whereby I am returned to ferve in Parliament, propofe, or give my confent to alter the Government, as it is fettled in one perfon and a Parliament.*

After which fubfcrption, the Members were admitted to affemble again; but not at all minding thofe things which the State expected at their hands, and on the contrary, inftead of cementing the commonalty in a perfect union; they fed them with vain and imaginary hopes, and endeavoured to difguft them with the Government: giving them to underftand, that they fhould enjoy happy dayes again, which they could not have hoped for till then, and which they were to expect from their confultations and affemblings. Wherefore his Highnefs having

having had patience with them full five entire
moneths, after he had several times exhorted
them to follow more lawful courses, and not
to forget their Duties by swerving from them in
such a manner as they did: But seeing all this
gained nothing upon their Spirits, his Highness
dissolved the Parliament on the tenth day of
January, 1655. five Moneths after its Convocation: and truly it was high time to put a period to their Consultation, which onely tended to
have ript up again the old sores of the State,
which his late Highness had so happily closed
up; and to have engaged *England* into a worse
Relapse then its former Mallady.

Parliament dissolved January 10. 1655.

And the venom and rancor which was hatched in the said Parliament was so general, that it
had spread it self through all the Counties of
England. Sir *Henry Littleton*, and Sir *John
Packington*, chief Actors in this Conspiracy, were
apprehended; and Major *Wildman* on the behalf of the Levellers was surprized and seized
on, as he was dictating a Paper to one of his
Servants, or rather a Libel, the Title whereof
was, *A Declaration containing the Motives and
Reasons which oblige us to take up Arms against
Oliver Cromwell.* Nor did this discovery at all
dishearten the Conspirators, the business being
so general, and so many People being engaged
therein, insomuch, that they ceased not to carry
on the Design, which they grounded more upon
the force then the fear thereof: and immediately News was brought, that a party of two hundred armed men had entred the Town of *Salisbury*.

Several Conspiracies discovered.

A Rising at Salisbury.

O

bury on Sunday about midnight, commanded by
Sir *Joseph Wagstaff,* *Penruddock,* and *Jones,* who
had been formerly Officers in the late Kings Army.   They presently seized on all the Inn, and
chief Houses; and whereas at that time the Af-
sizes were held at that place, they were so bold
as to take away the Judges Commissions and
Patents; and having likewise taken all their
Horses, they went away and marched towards
Pool.

A Rising
in *Shrop-*
shire.

At the same time a second party of these Ri-
sers did endeavour to surprize the Town and
Castle of *Shrewsbury,* but being discovered, their
design failed.

A Rising
in *Mont-*
gomery.

In *Montgomeryshire* eight hundred men got
to a head, which marching backwards and forwards, daily increased, and committed all kinde
of Acts of Hostility.

A Rising
in *Not-*
tingham-
shire.

There likewise came tydings from *Notting-*
hamshire, that a party of five hundred Horse had
been seen together in *Sheerwood Forest,* with
several Carts laden with Ammunitions; who
making an halt at an Inn which was scituated
from the Road, to consult on their Business,
were seized with a Pannick-fear: and no one of
their Enemies appearing or pursuing them, they
cryed out that they were betrayed; and so betook themselves to their heels, some one way
some another, in a confused manner.

A Rising
framing in
Northum-
berland.

So likewise did Collonel *Lilburn* send word
out of *Northumberland,* that they were busie in
framing of a party there also, but that they had
dissipated themselves through their own Fears
and Jealousies.   Finally,

Finally, in *Yorkshire*, Sir *Henry Slingsby*, and Sir *Richard Maleverer* had also assembled some Forces to have seized the City of *York*, having two Cart-loads of Ammunition with them; but they dispersed themselves on their own accompt, seeing but little appearance to succeed in their designe; Sir *Henry Slingsby* was taken and Imprisoned, and afterwards Beheaded upon another accompt.

A rising in Yorkshire.

The first party commanded by *Wagstaff* and *Penruddock* was defeated by Captain *Unton Crook*, at a place called *South-melton*; some whereof were killed and others were taken, who were Tried and Condemned; and those which dyed of note were Mr. *Lucas*, *Thorpe*, *Kensey*, *Graves*, and *Penruddock*, Sir *Joseph Wagstaff* had the hap to make his escape and to get away.

Wagstaff defeated and Penruddock and others executed.

Moreover a little afterwards to rid the State of such like Incendiaries and Firebrands, the several Prisons and Goals of *England* were delivered from the Royalists, which were detained prisoners on the foregoing accompts, who were sent away to the Plantations and Collonies in *America*.

Royalists sent to forreign Plantations.

In like manner, the rest of the other risings before mentioned, were quelled and dissipated, which both struck a terror in those who had not as yet shewn themselves, and restored peace and quietness to the State.

The Insurrections all dissipated.

By this time the subtil Spaniard, whose quaint policy doth for the most part hug the prosperous, and destroy the miserable and distressed,

A Spanish Ambassador sent over to his Highness

O 2   seeing

seeing that Fortune did daily more and more incline to favour his late Highness the Lord Protector; that his Vigour and Force increased by oppofition, and that the fole refplendency of his glory diffipated all thofe fogs and mifts which endeavoured to obfcure it, thought it meet to court *England*, and to endeavour to engage this State in his interefts, in which was omitted no proffers which a PuiffantMonarch could poffibly make unto a Prince, whofePower was but as it were in the bud, and beginning to fprout forth. To which purpofe the Marquis of *Leda* arived at *London* in the quality of an extraordinaryAmbaffador to his late Highnefs; where he was received with all the Demonftrations of Honour and Pomp. But his late Highnefs being over-fenfible of all thofe grofs injuries which the Spanifh Nation for feveral years together have committed againft the Englifh, and alfo againft all *Europe* befides; and being not willing to conforme his Maximes with the tyrannical and unjuft principles of the Spaniards, returned civil and ceremonious Anfwers to the faid Ambaffadors Propofals; who returned back again very fpeedily with all forts of contentment and fatisfaction, fave onely to that which he chiefly expected and moft of all infifted upon. And *England* being at that prefent time in a peaceable pofture, the Almighty having Crowned his late Highnefs the Lord protector with feveral fignal Victories and Deliverances of his perfon from an infinite number of Dangers, his Highnefs thought he could not in a better wife exprefs his acknowledgements

ments for so many mercies, then by the imploy-ing of all his Care and Forces to oppose and beat down the Ambition (nay I may justly say, their Sacraledge and Impiety) and Avarice of the Spaniards, since it onely belongs to a God to Stile himself the Universal Monarch; who at the expence and charge of an hundred thousand Murders and Devastations, have rendred them-selves Masters of the whole worlds Treasures. And withall, totally to extripate and root up the profound plots and devices which the Spa-niards had long since laid in *England* to become Masters thereof; or at least to breed divisions in it at their own pleasures. Nor shall I need to enlarge upon the ambitious and cruel designes of that invincible Armado of *Philip* the Second, which was to have invaded *England*, and to have made it swim in its own Blood; nor of those several entreagues and policies which *Spain* hath hatched in *Ireland*, by assistances of men and monies; as also by their several Conspira-cies in *England*, abusing of the Religion and blind zeal of some particular persons there: I shall onely begin with *Gundamore* that arch Ma-chiavilian Spanish Ambassador, who had gained such a Credit and Power in the Court of *Eng-land*; as that when he pleased he could dispose of the Lives of the greatest and best men in the State, when he had discovered they were his Ma-sters Enemies: I shall onely instance in one, that admirable personage Sir *Walter Rawleigh*, who by reason he had undertaken to visit their Treasures in *Hispaniola*, and had Committed

O 3   some

some hostillities in those Seas in former time, *Gundamore* never left importuning of *King James* (whom he had in a manner bewitched) till he had obtained his death, and thus bereaved *England* of one of the great Politicians and Universallest men that ever this Isle brought forth; leaving us a testimony of his vast knowledge and experience, to wit, his famous *History of the World*. From hence his late Highness resolved to begin his just War against the proud Spaniard, and to sacrifice to the memory of this great Captain (and one of the most experienced Sea-men of all the World) all the Spanish Blood which the valour of the noble English hath so generously by way of retaliation drawn and let out since his late Highness's expedition against them.

There are some friends with whom a man is forced to break off all friendship, because they will be too much our friends; that is, because they over-act the part of friendship by prying too deep into our Affairs and Designes, and by interesting themselves too far into the concernments of those who depend on us, as that thereby they steal away their hearts from us; and such like friends have the Spaniards been to *England*, who buy their friendships at such cheap rates, as that they feed those who side with them onely with imaginary speculations here on earth, making them eternally miserable; and with specious promises in the world to come, which would be obtained at cheaper and more assured rates without the interposing of their Hippocritical and Ambitious trains.　　　　But

But to return to our History again, his late Highness whose Genius affected the greatest difficulties, and the most extraordinary and rarest Designs, fix'd his thoughts upon *New Spain*; not to bereave them of their Treasures, which are with more ease to be interrupted at their coming home, but to revenge all *Europe*, unto whom the Jealous humor of the Spaniards denies Traffique and Commerce into those parts; having at all times exercised unheard of Cruelties and horrible Treacheries on such as were driven into those parts accidentally and forcibly by storms and tempests; or such as were by themselves, under the notion of friendship and kinde entertainment, drawn in thither to trade with them; whom they tyed stark naked unto trees, placing this Writing on their Breasts, *Who sent for you hither?* And in this wise suffered them to be eaten up alive by the Fowls of the Air, and the wilde Beasts of the Field.

And the better to accomplish this Design, on the twenty seventh of *December*, 1654. a gallant Fleet manned with brave Sea and Land-men, and well furnished with all kinde of Provisions and Ammunitions of War, set sail from *Portsmouth* Road under the Command of the Generals, *Penn* and *Venables*, upon a Design which was not made publick. On the first of *May* 1655. news was brought that they were arrived at the *Barbadoes* on the twenty-eight of *January*, where they had seized eighteen *Holland* Merchant-men, which traffiqued in those parts contrary to the Ordinance of the long Parliament;

The *Hispaniola* expedition

O 4 pro-

prohibitting the same. And by Letters of a fresher date, that they set sail from *Barbadoes* on the thirtieth of *March* towards *Hispaniola*. Where being arrived, by an unfortunate excess of prudence, the Commanders not deeming it fit to make a too near descent unto *Sancto Domingo* in *Hispaniola*, (which notwithstanding was deserted by all the Garrison at the very sight and appearance of so considerable a Fleet) landed their men somewhat lower; that so, during the time the Spaniards should come to impead their descent, they might have liberty to disimbark all their men, and to refresh themselves of the toils of the Sea. But this landing so far from the place, and deferring of the attempt, put a new life and courage into the Spaniards, who repossessed their place again; imagining that the English being unaccustomed to the excessive Heats of that Climate, and the deepness of the Sands, would be infinitely tyred in their March; and that by the said means they should be able to repulse and *withstand* them at a very cheap rate; which fell out just as the Spaniards had foreseen it: for the Climate was so hot and the Sands so deep, as that *the* English after their long march were not able to fight, were put to flight, and enforced to march back again to their ships; not without some difficulty; however, being seconded by fresh and valiant Sea-men, who went on shore to bring them off, they got on board again.

And that their long voyage and course might not prove totally useless and unprofitable, they resolved

resolved to set upon the Island of *Jamaica*, where they arrived on the tenth of *May* next ensuing; and after a little resistance which was made by the Spaniards, they became Masters of the place, which they have ever since preserved and kept with a great deal of constancy and glory, as we shall see hereafter.

Jamaica attempted and carried.

And that the English valour might be rendred more considerable and formidable to the whole World, the Almighty inspired into them that Religious Design, to revenge the Christians wrongs and sufferings against the Profanations and Abuses of the Turkish Barbarians, and crowned their pious attempt with as holy and glorious a Victory. Wherefore, General *Blake* having cast Anchor before *Tannis* on the eighteenth of *April*, 1655. sent unto the Dy of the place, to demand satisfaction for some English ships which the Pyrats of those parts had carried away, and the liberty of the English Slaves they had detained. But it was refused with scorn and derision, the Turks making this Answer, *Behold our Castles of Galetta, and our Castles and Vessels of Porto Ferino, do your worst against them, and do not think to brave us with the sight of your great Fleet.* Whereupon, General *Blake* being sensible, that the Glory of God, and the Honour of the English Nation was concerned in the punishing of so great a disdain; and to let the Enemies of Christ and Christianism see, *That they can do all things in and through him their strength and fortress*, he called a Councel of War, rather to implore the Almighties

General *Blake* demads satisfaction for wrongs sustained.

mighties affistance towards the compaffing of
fo glorious a Defign, then to refolve on the performing it. Each one finding himfelf animated
and armed with a more then naturall courage, to let thofe Infidels and all the World fee,
*That the Englifh are none of the leaft zealous in
the Concernments of Chrift* ; and fo joyntly refolved by all means poffible to burn hime of
their men of War which lay in *Porto Ferino*,
which was performed in the manner following.
The Sea-fhore was lined by one hundred and
twenty peeces of Cannon, and the Port was defended by the Caftle, on which twenty peeces
were mounted, befides fome other fmall Forts
which were alfo defended by great Guns and
Mufquet fhot. However, it was refolved, That
the Admiral, Vice-Admiral, and Rere-Admiral
fhould approach within mufquet fhot of the
Caftle, and there come to an Anchor, and in-
ceffantly fire upon the Caftle and other Forts,
whilft the reft of the Fleet fhould fecond and
back the Fire-fhips and long Boats which were
defigned to fire the Ships in the Port. And the
Almighty did evidently manifeft as well in the
hearts of the men, as by the blowing of the
Winde, that he bare a part in this undertaking ;
fo favourable was the Winde to the Englifh, and
fo much were their courages animated by his
Grace and Spirit : therefore in lefs then four
hours time the faid nine Ships were burnt down
to their very Keels, the Englifh for their part
lofing but five and twenty men which were flain,
and eight and forty wounded. Whereupon, the
King

General
Blake at-
tempts the
Turks for-
treffes and
navy.

King of *Tunis* sought to the English for their friendship, and restored all the Prisoners for little or nothing, amongst which divers Dutch also obtained their liberty amongst the English, not being distinguished by the Turks. And one of the English Admirals who went ashore to redeem the Captives, was highly honoured and treated, all which sufficiently recompensed the disdain they harboured against the Valour and Piety of the English.

Nor had these bold and glorious attempts sufficiently blazed the Vertue and Fortune of our late Protector, had they not continually been assailed by intestine Conspiracies which toss one on the back of the other, like unto so many Surges of the Sea, but which brake themselves in like manner upon a small shelf of Sand, on which the finger of God had worked their limits which they durst not exceed. Thus on the twelfth of *June* in the same Year, the Lords, *Willoughby* of *Parham*, and *Newport*, Mr. *Seamore*, and Mr. *Newport*, with some others, were sent Prisoners to the Tower of *London*, on suspicion of intermedling and assisting in a new Conspiracy. A fourth conspiracy suspected.

But to the end that evil might be repayed with good, and that the Sun might be heightned in its heat at the same time that the mists and fogs did thicken to obscure it, his Highness sent twelve good men of War, well manned, with Collonel *Humphreys* his Regiment to boot, and well provided with all necessaries, as well to reinforce the Naval Army as the Land Forces in *Jamaica*; A Relief sent to *Jamaica* in twelve ships.

Jamaica, which Fleet set sail on the second of *July* next ensuing, and in convenient space of time arived safely at their designed Port.

General *Pen* returns to *England*. Within a moneth after which, General *Pen* arrived in *England*, having left the best part of the Fleet in those parts under the Command of Vice-Admiral *Goodson*, a very valiant and experienced Sea-Commander, and the Troops which had mastered *Jamaica* under the Command of Collonel *Fortescue*. But as all prosperities are usually accompanied with some small Allayes of adversity, the Almighty suffering it to be so for our instruction and precaution, and to humble us in our highest transcendencies of Fortune; Wherefore the said Fleet having gained the height of the *Havennas* in the Isle of *Cuba*, the *Paragon* Frigot was fired by negligence, and perished in the flames with the greatest part of its Company and Mariners before she could be succoured or relieved.

General *Venables* also returned. On the ninth of the moneth of *September* ensuing, General *Venables* likewise returned from the Indies in the Frigot called the *Marston-moor*, in so weak and dejected a condition, that he was even at deaths door and nothing save the change of Air could possibly have saved him.

Treaty and Peace with *Sweden*. Mean while, the sympathy which all great and couragious persons seem to have for each other, begat a desire in his late Highness to be in amity with the King of *Sweden*, and likewise the King of *Sweden* on the other side coveted the same thing; so that the noble Lord *Bulstrode Whitlock*, one of Englands Worthies, having
                                               scarce

scarce his like for profound Knowledge and Sagacity, after he had resided for the space of eight Moneths in *Sweden*, terminated his Embassy by a compleat Peace and glorious Alliance, which he had concluded between that Crown and *England*; and returned himself to bring the good tydings thereof.

Now for the preservation of the Peace of this Commonwealth, his late Highness constituted several *Major-Generals* in the respective Counties thereof, whose Names are as followeth: viz.

1. For *Kent* and *Surrey*, Collonel *Kelsey*.

2. For *Sussex*, *Hamshire*, and *Barkeshire*, Collonel *Goff*.

3. For *Glocestershire*, *Wilts*, *Dorset*, *Somerset*, *Devon*, and *Cornwal*, General *Desborow*.

4. For *Oxfordshire*, *Bucks*, *Hertford*, *Cambridge*, *Isle* of *Ely*, *Essex*, *Norfolk*, and *Suffolk*, the Lord Deputy *Fleetwood*.

5. For the City of *London*, Major General *Skippon*.

6. For *Lincolnshire*, *Nottingham*, *Derby*, *Warwick*, and *Leicestershire*, Commissary General *Whaley*.

7. For *Northamptonshire*, *Bedford*, *Rutland*, and *Huntington*, Major *Butler*.

8. For *Worcester*, *Hereford*, *Salop*, and *North-Wales*, Collonel *Berry*.

9. For *Cheshire*, *Lancashire*, and *Staffordshire*, Collonel *Wortley*.

10. For *Yorkeshire*, *Durham*, *Cumberland*, *Westmerland*, and *Northumberland*, the Lord *Lambert*.

For

Major Generals constituted.

11. For *Westminster* and *Middlesex*, the Lieutenant of the Tower.

France seeks his Highness to perfect a Peace.

At this time *France* on her side being jealous of the several applications, profers, and propositions which the Spaniards made unto *England*, to beget an alliance with us, begun to be sensible that it was high time to think upon her owne preservation, her navigation being quite ruined, her subjects divided by Civil Wars, and intestine troubles, and her forreign Enemies as powerful as ever, resolved at length to make an addresse to his late Highness for an *Alliance of Peace*.

Reasons inducing his late Highness rather to condescend to an alliance with *France* then *Spain*.

Besides, that his late Highness harboured a natural averseness and hatred against the Spaniards, who time out of minde have alwayes been the implacable and cruel Enemies of *England*, as well as of all mankinde besides, and who under a fair pretence of Religion and Amity, endeavour to withdraw the Subjects of their Allyes, and make them swerve from their Allegiance and Fidelity, either by the powerful operations of money, gifts, and such like other bewitching inducements, rendring themselves the Masters of the peoples inclinations, when by their Valour they cannot overcome them in Battel, nor by force of Arms gain their Towns or Fortresses. But his late Highness open vertue and magnanimous courage disdaining any Commerce with this kinde of insinuating and entreaguing Nation, the Lion being too noble to enter into association and communication with the Fox; The French policy did better

jump

jump with his humor ; and their manner in vanquishing their Enemies in a pitch'd Battel, and foyling them upon the very Ramparts of their Fortresses, did better please and second his Warlike vertue ; and by whose good intelligence and communication, the English growing discipline could not choose but attain to a rare perfection; whereas the Spaniards might happily have poysoned them by their Wiles and Subtlties, and have corrupted them by their Hipocritical false Alloy and Mettal. Besides that the Liberty which is granted by the French to those who are of a different opinion in the points of Religion, was a great inducement to move his Highness rather to incline to a peace with that Nation, since himself was ever so tender in matters of Religion, as that he believed it did onely belong to the Almighty to fence the Consciences of Men, at least to enlighten and inspire them by his Graces, which are onely capable to convince our reason.

Finally, The Articles of peace with *France*, which were so much traversed by the Spanish Faction, were concluded and signed by such Commissioners as his late Highness had thereunto deputed ; and on the other part by his excellency the Lord *Bourdeaux* Ambassador of *France* : and on the eight and twentieth day of the moneth of *November* next ensuing, the publication of the said Treaty was proclaimed first at *White-hall* by the Heralds of Arms, the sound of Trumpets, and other formalities accustomed on the like occasions ; afterwards in the Palace-yard

A Peace with *France* Concluded and Proclaimed.

yard at *Westminster*, and in the other usual places in the City of *London* where such like Proclamations are made; and on the self-same day it was also published at *Paris* with a general applause and joy, at least of the Merchants, who by the preceding misunderstanding between *England* and *France* were quite ruined; and who by this conclusion of peace, found not onely the Seas open and free for them to trade in, but that the English of their worst Enemies became their best friends; by causing abundance to reign in their Rivers and Territories, and by begetting an assured Commerce and Navigation in all those Seas wherein the Navigation extended it self. Nor was the Lord Major of the City of *Paris* less glad then the poor Citizens, who all of them witnessed an equal joy and allacrity, finding themselves indulged by this Treaty of peace from breaking their Ember-weeks, their *Lent*, and Fasting dayes, (as they call them) since they would otherwise have been constrained (by reason of the excessive rates which fish, butter, and cheese, and such other small ratable wares were grown to) to have kept more fasting dayes then the *Roman Kallendar* doth enjoyn them; which would have been a double Penance and an intollerable mortification.

From all which they were freed by this happy Peace; and in acknowledgement whereof, the Guns and Chambers from the Market-place and Town-House called the *Greve*, as well as those from the *Bastile* or *Tower*, ecchoed forth the joy which the *Monsieurs* conceived of this forerunner

ner of the peace and tranquillity which they have since enjoyed in the heart of their Dominions, and the Victories and Conquests which they may yet atchieve by this happy Union, if their victorious and gallant Prince doth continue to accompany his Valour with those Vertues, which are onely capable not onely to give him addition of Crowns, but also to preserve them.

And lest I might insensibly out-slip my chief intent and purpose, and engage my self in the giving of you a Relation of the chiefest and most important Wars and Transactions of all *Europe*, should I recount unto you all the glorious Actions which have hapned since the Breach between *England* and *Spain*; in which our late Protector bare away all the share at Sea, and a very great part also by Land; as in our joynt Conquests in *Flanders*, and our particular ones in *Lorain*.

I shall therefore contract my pen a little, and onely give you a Breviate of the chiefest Actions, remitting the Reader to the more ample Histories both of *France* and *England*, to peruse the Relation of those Victories, wherewith Heaven hath blessed this Alliance for these late Years past: In which the mature deliberations and good Councels do more concern his late Highness, then the execution of those gallant Attempts which proceeded from them; although in truth both the one and the other may well be attributed to his great prudence, and to those Blessings which it hath pleased the Almighty to shower down upon his admirable

P good

good fortune, of which take some few Instances.

The defence and good success at *Jamaica*.

It is apparent to all the world in what a manner his late Highness provided for the preservation of *Jamaica*, notwithstanding all the force and attempts of *Spain* and the *Indies*, to free that Island again; although they never yet did set foot thereon, save to their own shame and confusion, having been driven thence again with the loss of all their Cannon and Baggage; and the which happened two several times, when as the Spaniards assembling all their Forces in the *Indies*, came and encamped themselves in the Island with two or three thousand men, had the time and opportunity to build and erect Forts, and for the space of some dayes to settle themselves: Notwithstanding which, the English as if they were but newly arrived from *England* to attempt a new Conquest of the Island, were constrained to imbark themselves and put to Sea again, the wayes being not passable by Land; and in that wise compassing the whole Island, they made their descent at the very place where the Enemies were encamped, and assailed them in their Forts and Breast-works with a far less number of men then theirs, and drave the Spaniards quite from them, and out of the Island, killing and taking several of their men, and retaining several of their great Guns and stately Standards as Trophies of their Victory.

General *Mountegue* his victory over the Spaniards at Sea.

Nor shall I enlarge upon that glorious Victory obtained by General *Mountegue* over the Spaniards at Sea, which was the first that made

this

this entrance into that famous War, and gave the Spaniards to understand, that it would cost them far more to transport their Gold from the *Indies* to *Spain*, then to dig it out of the Mines, or to refine it: The ensuing Poem penned by one of the most exquisite Wits of *England*, upon that subject, may better suffice to satisfie the Reader of the glorioufness of the Fact, and the shaming Stile which it is described by, is more proper to express this Heroick Action, then my low and unpolished Prose, which might haply obscure and detract from the luftre and splendor of so brave an Exploit; wherefore I have thought fit to insert the Poem it self.

Upon the present War with *Spain*, and the first Victory obtained at Sea.

Now for some Ages had the pride of Spain,
Made the Sun shine on half the World in vain;
While she bid War, to all that durst supply
The place of those, her Cruelty made dye.
  Of Nature's Bounty men forbare to tafte,
And the best Portion of the Earth lay wafte.
From the New World, *her Silver and her Gold,*
Came like a Tempeft, to confound the Old:
Feeding with these the brib'd Elector's Hopes,
She made at pleasure Emperors and Popes:
With these, advancing her unjuft Defigns,
Europe was shaken with her Indian Mines.
  When our Protector looking with disdain
Upon this gilded Majefty of Spain;

P 2   *And*

And knowing well that Empire must decline,
Whose chief support, and sinews, are of Coyn:
Our Nation's sollid vertue, did oppose
To the rich Troublers of the World's repose.

And now some moneths encamping on the Main,
Our Naval Army had besieged Spain.
They that the whole Worlds Monarchy design'd,
Are to their Ports by our bold Fleet confin'd:
From whence our Red Cross they triumphant see,
Riding without a Rival on the Sea.
Others may use the Ocean as their road,
Onely the English make it their abode:
Whose ready Sails with every Winde can flie,
And make a covenant with th'unconstant Skie.
Our Oaks secure, as if they there took root;
We tread on Billows with a steady foot.

Mean while the Spaniards in America,
Near to the Line, the Sun approaching saw;
And hop'd their European Coasts to find
Clear'd from our ships, by the Autumnal Winde.
Their huge capacious Gallions stuft with Plate,
The laboring winds drives slowly towards their fate.

Before Saint Lucar they their Guns discharge,
To tell their Joy, or to invite a Barge.
This heard some Ships of ours, though out of view,
As swift as Eagles to the quarry flew.

So heedless Lambs which for their mothers bleat,
Wake hungry Lions, and become their meat.
Arriv'd, they soon begin that Tragick play,
And with their smoakie Cannon banish day:
Night, horror, slaughter, with confusion meets,
And in their sable Arms imbrace the Fleets.

Through

Through yielding Planks the angry Bullets fly,
And of one Wound hundreds together dye.
Born under different Stars, one Fate they have,
The Ship their Coffin, and the Sea their Grave.

    Bold were the men, which on the Ocean first
Spread their new Sails, whilst shipwrack was the
More danger now from men alone we find, (worst,
Then from the Rocks, the Billows, or the Wind.
They that had sail'd from near th' Anartick Pole,
Their Treasure safe, and all their Vessels whole,
In sight of their dear Countrey ruin'd be,
Without the guilt of either Rock or Sea.
What they would spare, our fiercer Art destroyes,
Excelling storms, in terror and in noise.

    Once Jove *from* Hyda *did both Hoasts survey,*
And when he pleas'd to Thunder, part the Fray :
Here Heaven in vain that kinde Retreat should
The louder Canon had the thunder drown'd. (sound,

    Some we made Prize while others burnt & rent,
With their rich Lading to the bottom went.
Down sinks at once (so Fortune with us sports)
The Pay of Armies, and the Pride of Courts.

    Vain man, whose rage buries as low that store,
As Avarice had digg'd for it before.
What Earth in her dark bowels could not keep
From greedy hands, lies safer in the Deep :
Where Thetis *kindly doth from mortals hide,*
Those seeds of Luxury, Debate, and Pride.
And now into her lap the richest Prize
Fell, with the Noblest of our Enemies.

    The Marquis *glad to see the fire destroy*
Wealth, that prevailing Foes were to enjoy :

Out

Out from his flaming Ship his Children sent,
To perish in a milder Element,
Then laid him by his burning Ladies side,
And since he could not save her, with her dy'd.
Spices and Gums about them melting fry,
And Phœnix-like, in that rich nest they dye.
Death bitter is, for what we leave behinde,
But taking with us, all we love, is kinde.
VVhat could he more then hold for term of life,
His Indian Treasure, and his more priz'd VVife ?
Alive, in flames of equal Love, they burn'd,
And now together are to ashes turn'd.
Ashes more worth, then all their Funerals cost,
Then the huge Treasure which was with them lost.
    These dying Lovers, and their floating Sons,
Suspend the Fight, and silence all our Guns.
Beauty and Youth, about to perish, findes
Such noble pitty in brave English mindes ;
That the rich Spoil neglecting, and the Prize,
All labour now to save their Enemies.
    How frail our Passion's ? how soon changed are
Our wrath and fury to a friendly care ?
They that but now to gain the Spanish Plate,
Made the Sea blush with Blood, forget their Hate;
And their young Foes, while sinking, they retrive,
VVith greater danger then they fought, they dive.
    VVith these returns Victorious Mountague,
VVith Laurel in his hands, and half Perue.
    Let the brave General divide that bough,
    Our great Protector hath such Wreaths enough.
His conquering Head hath no more room for Bayes,
Then let it be as the whole Nation prayes :

                                    Let

Let the rich Oare forthwith be melted down,
And the State fixt, by making him a Crown:
With Ermins clad, and Purple; let him hold
A Royal Scepter, made of Spanish Gold.

Take the particulars of the Fight briefly thus: The Spaniards were seven in number, richly laden, about nine Leagues from *Cadiz*, coming from the West Indies; one whereof was burnt, another sunk, two run aground, two were taken, one got away, with a *Portugal* Prize. In the ship that was burnt, was the Marquis of *Badex*, his Wife, and one Daughter. In one of the ships taken, was the young Marquis his Brother, and another Sister, who was set on shore in *Spain*. The two Brothers were brought to *England* with a great deal of wealth.

And amongst these Victories which were gained at Sea against the Spaniards since the breach of the Peace, that which was obtained by General *Blake* at *Sancta Cruza*, in the Island of *Teneriff*, on the twentieth day of *April*, 1657. was none of the least; in which Port there was sixteen great Vessels burnt and sunk by the English; and the Spaniards Forts and Castles of the Isle, amidst which there were five or six great Gallions, the Admiral, Vice-Admiral, and Rere-Admiral, the greatest part whereof were mounted with Brass Ordnance, and laden some with rich merchandizes from the Indies, and the others with provisions and other manufactures to be transported thither, equipied in ample manner both with Soldiers and Mariners.

General *Blakes* destroying the Spanish Fleet at the Canaries.

P. 4   All.

All which having their Flags, Ensignes, and Streamers flying, were set upon by the English, who in less then four hours time destroyed them all without the loss of above sixty men; the greatest part of which were killed by the Musquet shot which played from the shoar: But in lieu of them, the English with their Cannon killed a great number of the Spaniards in their Breast-works and Forts.

Wherefore his late Highness who never recompensed vertuous and magnanimous actions which bare praise, sent a civil Letter of thanks to General *Blake*, with a Diamond Ring valued at five hundred pounds, and gave the Captain that brought the news one hundred pound for a present. Moreover, according to his accustomed Piety, he ordained a day of publick Prayer and Thanksgiving to be set apart, to return all Thanks, Acknowledgements, Praise, and Glory to the Almighty, for this so happy and signal a success; and to supplicate his Divine *Bounty* to bestow frequent and like Blessings upon the English Armadoes and Land Forces.

But the Sea being a Theater or Stage too unstable for so settled a valour and constant a Fortune, the traces and marks which she receives of Combates and Victories are too soon worn out, and scarce leave unto History, and to the memory of men, wherewith to raise Monuments, erect Triumphs, and to transmit unto posterity the truth of things; and although that vertue be the more glorious, by how much the greater dangers it assails and surmounts; yet

how-

however, as a flight is more eafily made by Sea then by Land , where feldome men fight at hand-blows, we have reafon to give the firft praife and honour to that Element which firft brought us forth, and whence we reap the moft beneficial neceffaries towards our fubfiftence. In like manner, his late Highnefs's folid policy was imployed on fuch folid foundations where it might lay deep rooting, and fpread its large branches far and near without the apprehenfion of being fapped or dug up.

The French therefore being defirous to be re-venged for their ill fuccefs at *Valenchenes*, re-folved the next fummer to affault *Montmedy*, a ftrong Frontier feated upon a Rock ; but being not ftrong enough to keep the Spaniards in play in *Flanders* , they feparated part of their Army to profecute the faid fiege ; and the Englifh began to make their firft landing in *Flanders,* Sir *John Reynolds,* was chofen by his late High-nefs to command the Body of the Englifh For-ces, confifting in fix thoufand Foot, who happily landed in *Picardy* about the latter end of *May.* And that it may not feem to be a digreffion from my fubject, I fhall omit the particulari-zing of the fiege, and the taking of *Montmedy,* and fhall onely tell you, that the Marfhal *De la Ferte,* who carried on that fiege, was not at all incommodated by the Enemy from without , during the whole fiege ; nor durft the Spaniard ever fet upon the French Army, thereby to at-tempt the relief of that place. And although it would be a piece of injuftice to difpoil that war-
like

May. 4. 1657. The Englifh joyn with the French in *Flan-ders* un-der Sir *John Rey-nolds.*

like nation of their glory, yet all men know that their Army wanted Foot extreamly that Summer; but the English foot (which we must confess is the best in all *Europe*) being joyned to their Cavalrie, (which also excel all others) there had not a more resolute and gallant Army been seen in *France* for many years together.

And here by the way take notice of the Installment of his late Highness in the Protectorship, which was on this manner, *viz.* On the twentieth day of the moneth of *June*, in the year of our Lord God 1657. being appointed for the Installment of his late Highness the Lord Protector; a large and spacious place was raised at the upper end of *Westminster-Hall* under the great window, in the midst whereof, a Rich Cloath of State was set up, and under it a Chair of State was placed upon an ascent of two degrees, covered with Carpets; before which stood a Table with a Chair appointed for the Speaker of the Parliament. On each side of the Hall, upon the said Structure there were seats raised one above each other, and decently covered for the Members of the Parliament; and below them there were Seats made for the Judges of the Land on the one side, and for the Aldermen of the City on the other side.

About two of the Clock in the afternoon, his Highness met the Parliament in the Painted Chamber, and passed such Bills as were presented to him; after which they went in order to the place appointed in *Westminster-Hall*: his Highness being entred on the place, and standing
ing

ing under the Cloath of State, Mr. Speaker did in the Name of the Parliament, present several things which lay ready on the Table, unto his Highness, *viz.*

A Robe of Purple Velvet, lined with Ermines, being the habit, anciently used at the solemn Investure of Princes; next a large Bible richly Gilt and Bossed, and lastly a Scepter of massie Gold, which being thus presented, Mr. Speaker came from his Chair, took the Robe and therewith vested his Highness, being assisted by the Earl of *Warwick*, the Lord *Whitlock*, and by others; which being done, the Bible was delivered to his Highness; after which Mr. Speaker girt about him the Sword; and finally delivered his Highness the Scepter; which being thus performed, Mr. Speaker returned to his Chair, and administred the Oath to his Highness which had been prepared by the Parliament for him to take.

His Highness standing thus adorned in Princely State, Mr. *Manton*, by prayer recommended his Highness Forces by Sea and Land, the whole Government and People of these Nations, to the blessing and protection of God Almighty.

After which, the people gave several shouts, and the Trumpets sounding, his Highness sate down in the Chair of State, holding the Scepter in his hand; and whilst his Highness thus sate, a Herald of Arms stood aloft, making a signal to a Trumpet to sound three times; after which, by direction and Authority of Parliament, he did there publish and proclaim his Highness, *Oliver*
Lord

Lord *Cromwel,* Lord Protector *of* England, *Scotland, and* Ireland, *and the* Dominions *thereto belonging.* Hereupon the Trumpets sounded again and the People gave several Acclamations, with loud shouts, crying, *God save the Lord Protector.*

After a little pause, the Ceremony being ended, his Highness saluting the Ambassadors, and publick Ministers, proceeded thence in his Princely Habit, (the Train whereof was born up by six noble persons) and passed through the Hall into the Palace-yard, the Earl of *Warwick,* carrying the sword before him, *where his* Highness entred into his Coach, attended by his Life-guards and Halberdeirs; the Officers of State; the Lord Major and Aldermen; all which waited on his Highness back to *Whitehall*; the whole Ceremony having been managed with State and Magnificence, suitable to so high and happy a Solemnity.

Mardike taken by the English and French.

But to return to our History again, toward the end of the Summer therefore, the united Forces of *England* and *France* took the Fort of *Mardike,* whereof Major General *Morgan* took possession for the English, as the earnest of further Conquests. The Spaniard hereupon conceived all the fears and jealousies which so dangerous a neighbour-hood might justly cause, which obliged them in the following moneth to resolve vigorously to assault the place, and to

The Spaniards repulst at Mardike.

carry it by force: But they were received with so much vigour by the English, as that they were manfully beaten off, and constrained to retire with a great loss of their men, and of several Officers of note.   But

But the joy of these successes were modera-
ted by the death of Admiral *Blake*, a person
who had so well deserved of *England*, as that
he may be justly intituled its *Neptune*, at the
same time when as his Highness was its *Jupiter*
and *Mars*; who caused him to be buried with
all the Demonstrations of Honour due to his
high demerits. He came within sight of *Plimou*th
onely to give up the Ghost, and received this
satisfaction at his death, to have bestowed all
the Moments of his life on that Element which
had given him so much glory; just like unto
Moley Moluch that Illustrious King of *Fess*,
who at the Article of Death, caused himself to
be carried in a Litter into his Camp, where
he expired in the middle of the Battel, as he was
exhorting his Soldiers, and gained the Victory.
In like manner dyed General *Blake* in the midst
of his famous Combats and Victories, regret-
ed by all *England*; and his late Highness, who
had alwayes an especial care to cause those honours to be rendred to such great persons as
were due to their demerits, would have him
stately interred, as the Earl of *Essex* had been
before; but General *Blakes* body was onely
brought with a Naval Pomp by Water in State
on the *Thames* from *Greenwich* to *Westminster*,
as being a more suitable Ceremony to his imployment; and was there buried in *Henry* the
Seventh's famous Chappel.

Now the Spaniards disgusted at the firme
footing the English had both gotten and kept
at *Mardike*, conceiving that against the next
Spring

Spring it might give them a greater in-let in *Flanders*, deemed they had best to endeavour the driving of them thence betimes, before they should be too well settled and established there; they resolved to assault them again, and accordingly did set upon them very vigorously and resolutely with a party very considerable, commanded by the pretended Princes of *Holyland*, and the Marquis of *Coracene*; but the English defended themselves so manfully and stoutly, as that the Spaniards began to judge that as the French are good at taking of places, so the English were constant in keeping and defending them; insomuch as that my *Dons* were forced to return by weeping cross to *Dunkirk*, and take their last farewell of *Mardike.*

For they might very well have perceived by the business of St. *Venant*, that the English were as good at the one as at the other; when as the Spaniards having besieged *Ardres*, the English supposed that their advance into *France* was onely to retard their progress into *Flanders*, gave so resolute an assault to St. *Venant*, as that they carryed the place and had the sole honour of it; and immediately marching towards *Ardres*, they drove away the Spaniards then with so much courage and resolution as amazed the French. Wherefore this latter part of the season having been imployed in sowing the seeds of those *Laurels* which they were to reap in the next years expedition in *Flanders*. His late Highness recollected himself, to establish Peace and Tranquility in *England*, and to

fettle

settle the foundation of a happy and glorious
Government.

And deeming that he could not more justly
confer the eminent dignities of the Land, save The Lord
upon those who together with their blood had *Henry*
sucked from him the seeds and buds both of Mi- *Cromwel*
litary and Politick Vertues; he created his made de-
younger son the Lord *Henry Cromwel*, Lord De- puty of
puty of *Ireland*; who hath alwayes and doth *Ireland*.
still behave himself with so much conduct and
applause in this so eminent a charge, as that envy it self is constrained to confess, that his Fathers wisdome could not have made a better
choice.

Much about this time the Officers at *Mar-*
dike, in whose breasts the rigour of the winter
did onely excite the heat of those designs which
they had conceived in their souls, being desirous
to imploy part of that unprofitable season to
concourse and consult that Oracle of Prudence,
who by the conduct of their Heroick Projects
did inspire into them the vertue and efficacy to
compass their designs, and to surmount even the
greatest difficulties, Sir *John Reynolds*, I say, Sir *John*
Commander in chief, Collonel *White*, and some *Reynolds*
other Officers, being impatient to enjoy the and others
happiness of seeing and consulting his High- drowned.
ness, embarqued at *Mardike* for *England*; but
the mischance was, that being assailed by a tempest, they were unfortunately cast away upon the
Goodwin Sands, and so frustrated all the world
of the expectations of those fair hopes which
were conceived of their valours, and of so fortu-
nate beginnings. On

On the fourth day of the moneth of *February* then next enfuing, his late Highnefs repaired to the Lords Houfe then in Parliament, and having fent notice thereof to the Houfe of Commons by the Keeper of the Black-Rod, the Speaker with the Members came to the Lords Houfe, where ftanding without the Bar, and his Highnefs within under a Cloath of State, being animated with his wonted vigour and refolution, fuccinctly told them without many preambles, That it concerned his Intereft as much as the publike Peace and Tranquility, to terminate this Parliament, fo that he was come thither to diffolve the fame, which was alfo immediately performed.

On the twelfth day of the moneth of *March* enfuing, his late Highnefs being defirous to oblige the City of *London* in a particular manner, and at the fame time to witnefs unto them the care he took for their prefervation and tranquillity; he fent for the Lord Major, the Aldermen, and the other Magiftrates of the City, and having made them fenfible of his tendernefs and care for their good, he alfo reprefented unto them, that during the Calm, Tempefts were moft of all to be apprehended: fo that at fuch times, the requifite Orders and neceffary preventions to refift Troubles, were to be chiefly minded. For to this knowing and vigilant Spirit, to whom nothing was dark or hid; this penetrating Light, who could pry even into mens hearts; and who from out of his Cabinet could difcover the moft fecret Plots which were

hatching

The Parliament diffolved Febr.4. 165⅞

The City Militia fettled again by his late Highnefs.

hatching throughout all *Europe*, declared unto them, That the Enemies both of the State and of their City did not sleep, although it seemed they were quite lulled: That their City was great and vaste, and like unto a corpulent Body, nourished several ill humours: That he requested them for their own goods to have a special care, and to bear a watchful eye: That he relied much upon their Vigilancy and Affection, and that all he could contribute thereunto on his behalf, was to re-establish the City *Militia*, (which had been abolished through the disorder of the foregoing Wars) and to desire them to appoint for their Officers, persons of Honour and Probity, well-wishers and friends to the peace and quietness of the State and publique Good. Whereupon, the Lord Major and Officers having returned thanks to his Highness for so signal a Mark of his confidence and goodness towards them, proceeded to settle the *Militia*, and repayed him with all the Obedience and Fidelity, which a Magnanimous Prince could expect from Subjects, who were well versed in the duties they owed to a Governour, who had rid them of a world of miseries, and delivered them from the burthen of a Civil War.

Nor was this precaution or forewarning of his late Highness without some grounds or foundation; for on the twenty fourth of the said Moneth, the quiet Serpent which hatched its poison under the green grass, unawares let slip a Hiss, whereupon an exact search was made throughout all *London* and *Westminster* for suspected

A Conspiracy discovered

Q

pected persons, divers of which were secured and imprisoned. His late Highness knowing full well, that States are maintained, as well by Justice as by force of Arms, and that those chiefly stand in need of both, which through the divisions of Mens mindes, touching Spiritual concernments, seem to be in a continual apprehension of those revolutions, which at all times have been caused in the World by the means of these diversities of opinions. His Highness I say through the cause of these apprehensions, and the discoveries which were already made, as aforesaid, caused a High Court of Justice to be erected, according as it had been decreed by an Act of Parliament, and settled under the great Seal of *England*: and truly it was high time for the Swords of Justice to appear to chastise the Conspirators, since the sparkles of their fury had spread themselves abroad through its veil, rather by their immoderate heat then their sad looks; *several persons* of quality were imprisoned in the Tower of *London*; and within few dayes afterwards, just like unto a River, which is ready to disgorge it self into the Sea, appears great and violent at its entrance, so also the Conspiracy being just ready to break forth, appeared the more formidable; and assured there were whole Regiments enrolled, and in the midnight of *May-day* they should have set fire on several parts of the City, and whilest the confusion and horror thereof had seized all men, they should have made a general Massacre of all those who would have

A high Court of Justice erected.

have opposed their fury. His Highness like
unto the Sun, elevated up to the highest Heaven, peirced through all those other Sphears,
which were darkned to all other Lights but his,
and dissipated those Fogs and Mists, which the
darkness of the Furies had spread over the City
of *London*; for on the morning of that fatal
intended day, the Guards were doubled both
within and without the City; and about five of
the Clock in the Evening, both Horse and Foot
were drawn up in Arms; the City Militia likewise keeping strong Guards all that night, to
prevent and hinder so sad and horrid an attempt. Mean while, all care was taken to difcover the Firebrands before they could enter
upon their exploit; and as Enterprizes wherein so many persons are engaged cannot remain
very secret or hidden, about seven of the Clock
that Evening, about forty of the Conspirators
were taken and carried to *White-Hall*, and on
the day following, several others of all kindes
and conditions were also apprehended; as
Gentlemen, Merchants, Souldiers, and the like;
many of which were condemned to dye as Traytors: but his late Highness was so merciful to
pardon the most part of them, to the end that
like unto a second *Augustus* he might gain by
his Clemency those hearts which would not be
mollified by the horror of the undertakings,
nor the rigour and severity of the punish-
ments.

> The Plot prevented

> Several Conspira-
> tors taken
> and sen-
> tenced,
> some con-
> demned,
> others par-
> doned.

On the second day of the moneth of *June* then
next ensuing, there arrived a strange accident on
the

the *Thames* near *London*, to wit, a Whale of a prodigious bigness, at least sixty foot, and of a proportionable breadth, was cast up. This great Fish, which may be stiled the King of the Sea for his bulk, came to do homage to his late Highness, and by his Captivity and Death, to to let him see he was absolute Master of that terrible Element which had given her a being.

But let us again return to the Wars in *Flanders*, and let us see how whole Armies and Cities do there submit unto his Highness power, as well as the Sea Monsters here. Now although taking and keeping of *Mardike* had been a sufficient warning to the Spaniards to provide the Town of *Dunkirk* with all necessaries to withstand a Siege, however that changed not the English their resolution to attempt it; wherefore the United Forces both of *France* and *England*, under the Command of those two glorious Chieftains, his Highness the Martial of *Tureine*, Prince of *Quesnoy*, and his Excellency the Lord Ambassador and General *Lockhart*, besieged the place, opened the approaches, and with an incredible diligence perfected the Circumvolution.

The Spaniards intending to attempt the relief of the place, being the Key of all *Flanders*, and the chief Sea Port, assembled all their Forces, and made up a considerable Army of sixteen thousand men, with a design to have forced the Lines, and to have raised the Siege. To which intent, on the third of *June* they came in a Body through *Fuernes*, and encamped within an English mile and a half of the Martial

Tureines

Turaines Quarters; who being aware of their intent, the following night brake up his Camp, and having left part of his Forces to make good the Approaches, and to guard the Trenches, marched all night with fifteen thousand men and ten peeces of cannon to encounter the Enemy, to decide in a pitched Battle and an open Field, with an equal advantage, which party should be victorious.

The English Foot drawn up into four great Battalions, and led on by his Excellency the Lord Ambassador and General *Lockhart*, gave the first on-set upon five great Battalions of the Spanish Foot placed very advantagiously on three high and great Downs, seconded by *Don John* of *Austria* himself, and the best of the Spanish and Condean Forces, which they had purposely opposed unto the English, conceiving them to have been as yet Novices in the manner of waging War beyond Seas, and that for want of Discipline and Conduct they would soon have been routed and disordered : But they were suddenly deceived in their expectations, and found that they had to deal with persons of courage and resolution, who as well in the Military Discipline, as in the Art of Courtship, became perfect and absolue Masters even during their first years of Apprenticeship; wherefore it was not without reason the Ancients did alwayes joyn *Mars* and *Venus* together, since towards the doing of gallant Actions, it is sufficient to be passionate and resolute at the very entering into the Lists of either of these Divinities.   The

Q 3   English

English therefore affailing the Spaniards in their advantageous ftand as aforefaid, in the high Downs, did themfelves alone feverall times charge them, and fuftained both the Brunt of their Horfe and Foot, without ever being feconded or relieved by the French; who were fo confident of their Refolution and Valour, as that they would not feem to intreach upon their Honour; befides that, they were loath to change their Stands, leaft thereby they might bring themfelves into a diforder: and finally, forcing the Spaniards to quit their ftations, they put them to a total rout and confufion. In which Charge up the Downs, Lieutenant Collonel *Fenwick*, who fhewed a great deal of Gallantry in leading on his Excellency the Lord Ambaffador and General *Lockharts* Regiment of Blue, received his mortal wound by a Mufquet Bullet through the Body, whereof he dyed fome few dayes after. Divers other perfons of quality and note fighallized themfelves not a little that day at the Head of their refpective Regiments; as the Honorable Collonel *Lillingfton*, Lieutenant Collonel *Fleetwood*, Captain *Devaux*, who led up a Forelorn of three hundred Mufquetiers, and gave the firft Charge upon the Spaniards: And of the Voluntiers, Collonel *Henry Jones*, who at firft charged with Lieutenant Collonel *Fenwick* on foot, afterwards on Horfeback, when as engaging too far, he was taken prifoner, but was afterwards exchanged; and by his late Highnefs at his return into *England*, made Knight and Baronet. Divers others did gallantly, who

doubtlefs

The Spaniard beaten by the English and French

doubtless will not be forgotten in the English Annals, and would be too large to be expressed in this Epitome relating onely to his Highness.

The Spaniards had at first resolved to have given no English man quarter, but the fortune of the day made them glad to seek to the English for quarter themselves ; and it was well they could have it given them, although the English were generous enough to have spared their Lives, had not the zeal of overcoming, and their resolutions to perfect the Victory, taken up all their care and passions. Finally, the Spanish Foot being totally routed, and coming to surrender themselves to the English in whole troops, the English mistrusting they had some other intentions and stratagem thereby, neither understanding their Language nor designe, continued charging them, and enforced them to seek quarter elsewhere, preferring the gaining of the Victory to their own particular interests ; and so reaped an intire glory in their despising and rejecting several prisoners of quality, who profered themselves to them, and for the which they might have had considerable ransoms.

And in the gaining of those high Downs on which the Spaniards were placed, the English behaved themselves with so much gallantry and resolution, as that envy and malice raised a report amidst the jealous and their Corivals, that it savoured more of a piece of rashness then of a true valour ; as if Soldiers could possibly with too much zeal and readiness performe those Commands which are given them.

To

To be brief, the victory wholly declared it
self for the English and for the French, and the
whole Spanish Army was quite discomfited and
pursued to the very Gates of *Fuernes*, with the
loss of three thousand five hundred men, two
thousand whereof were killed on the place of
Suydcote, a Village seated in the Downs between
Dunkirk and *Fuernes* ; and the rest were taken
prisoners, and the whole Army dissipated and
disordered : which defeat having quite disheartned the besieged, and depriving them of all
hopes of relief, besides their Govornour the Marquis *De Leda* being mortally wounded by two
hand Granadoes as he defended the false bray,
and of which wounds he dyed, constrained them
to beat a Parley fourteen dayes afterwards, and
to surrender the place on the fifteenth of *July*
1658. after the one and twentieth day of the
opening of the Approaches. And in this man-

**Dunkirk
taken and
possessed
by the
English.**

ner this famous Sea-port was reduced under
the obedience of his late Highness the Lord Protector, and was by the French put into the
hands of his Excellency the Lord Ambassador
and General *Lockhart*, who was by his Highness declared Governour of the same ; and took
possession of it with four English Regiments
which compose the Garrison thereof, and serve
to defend the Fort *Mardike*, and the new Fort
Royal, begun by the Spaniards on the Channel
of *Burges*, and perfected by the English, now
called *Olivers* Fort. The Inhabitants of which
place are so much taken with the superabundan-
cy of the generosity and goodness of their said
Go-

Governour his Excellency the Lord *Lockhart*, as that they repent themselves to have so much listned to the Spanish false perswasions and fears, which they possessed them with, that they should be cruelly and inhumanely treated by the English, purposely to make them resist the longer. It had been well they had had so much care of their Souls, as they perswaded them they had of their Goods and Fortunes.

But it would be too great a conquest to pretend joyntly to overcome both the Consciences of men and their Town to boot; the first is Gods due, and the other *Cæsars*. And we may observe in *Alexander* the Great, whensoever his Forces became Masters of any place, he would alwayes sacrifice to the Gods of the Countrey; thereby to gain the Inhabitants hearts, and to induce their Gods to become propitious to him. *Numa Pompilius* was a King before he was a Priest, and although the Almighty hath imprinted in all men a particular inclination to adore him, yet however as concerning the manner of worshipping him, Policy alwayes preceded Religion, and ever kept the upper hand over her as much as she possibly could.

King *Henry* the Fourth of *France* was a Protestant whilst he had overcome his Enemies, but as soon as he was settled in the Throne, and that he was to Reign as King, he seemingly returned Papist, and said, *That the Kingdome of France and City of Paris was worth a going to Mass.* But when as superstitious and zealous spirits counselled him to prosecute and pursue the Protestants ftants, he anfwered, *That fo long as they remained faithful and true to him, and continued to ftand by and ferve him as they were wont, he would be as much a Father and Protector unto him, as unto the reft of his good Subjects.* Thefe Maximes are general and common, and admit of no diftinctions fave in Schools; nor need the Spaniards with all their Hypocrifie and Pious malice to doubt, but that *France* and *England* underftanding each other well enough, and that the Englifh themfelves are prudent enough to avoid that which may prejudice them, and to tollerate whatfoever may advance and further their conquefts, and beget a love and efteem of their government. But to return to our former fubject again, as we have oft before alledged, the joyes of this World are alwayes for the moft part mingled with fome allayes of forrow; the Almighty being willing to keep us mindful that there are no perfect felicities to be enjoyed here on earth; and that its onely in heaven we are to expect an intire and perpetual Contentment and Blifs. Wherefore the *Laurels* of the Victory obtained againft the Spaniards, and of the taking of the Town of *Dunkirk* were foon withered, and the joyes abated, by the interpofing of the Cyprefs-tree which death planted upon the

Tomb of the Illuftrious and moft generous Lady

The Lady Cleypolls death.

Cleypoll, fecond Daughter to his late Highnefs, who departed this mortal life to a more glorious and eternal one on the fixth day of *Auguft* this prefent year: a fatal prognoftication of a more fenfible enfuing lofs. For even as Branches of
Trees

trees being cut and lopped in an ill season, do first draw away the sap from the tree, and afterwards cause the body thereof to dry up and dye; In like manner, during the declining age of his late Highness, an ill season, in which men usually do as it were reap all their consolation from the youth and vigor of their Children, wherein they seem to ruine by degrees as they draw near to their death, it unfortunately fell out, that this most illustrious Daughter, the true representative and lively Image of her Father, the Joy of his Heart, the Delight of his Eyes, and the Dispenser of his Clemency and Benignity, dyed in the flower of her age, which struck more to his Heart then all the heavy burthens of his Affairs, which were onely as a pleasure and pastime to his great Soul. So great a power hath Nature over the dispositions of generous Men, when the eye of Blood is seconded by love and vertue. This generous and noble Lady *Elizabeth* therefore departed this World in despite of all the skill of Physicians, the Prayers of those afflicted persons whom she had relieved, and the vows of all kinde of Artists whom she cherished. But she dyed an Amazonian-like death, despising the Pomps of the Earth, and without any grief, save to leave an afflicted Father perplex'd at her so sudden being taken away; she dyed with those good Lessons in her mouth, which she had practised whilest she lived. And if there be any comfort left us in her death, it is the hope we have, That her good Example will raise up the like inclinations in the remain-
der

der of her Sisters whom Heaven hath yet left us.
I shall not at all speak of her Funerals, for if I
might have been credited, all the Muses and
their God *Apollo*, should have made her an *Epicedium*, and should have appeared in mourning,
which should have reached from the top of their
Mount *Parnassus* to the bottom of the valley
thereof.   But if this illustrious Personages death
received not the Funeral Rites which all great
Wits were bound to pay it, at least the Martial
men did evidence, that the disgrace lay not at
their doors, but that they ought to reap all the
glory, since they were not backward to continue
to brave and affront dangers in the behalf of an
illustrious and glorious Cause: wherefore the
sad tydings of this noble Personages death
touched the gallant English to the heart, seeing
they were bereaved of their English *Pallas*, and
of their *Jupiters* Daughter; they therefore accused the Destinies for intrenching upon their Priviledges, and evidenced, that it appertained not
alone unto them to dispose of the lives of men.
Their wrath therefore discharged it self on the
first Objects which presented themselves to their
eyes: and the harmless Spaniards were so many
Victims offered up to this *Amazons* shrine; and
as if *Graveling* had been her stake, they were so
eagerly bent to fire the Enemies out of the same,
as that the Spaniards were constrained to open
their gates to give vent to the fire and flame
which suffocated them, and surrendered themselves to the Conquering French Army; to
whose share that place fell, and by whose force it
was solely gained.   As

*Graveling
taken by
the French*

As Phyficians do agree that extreme Joy cau-feth Death as well as exceffive Grief, fo may we likewife fay, That both thefe violent Paffions united together, muft needs deftroy the ftrong-eft perfon on earth; and that the Conflict which they produce in a Soul, is capable to turn the edge of the keeneft weapons which are op-pofed to their refiftance, and to make the faireft champain Field become a parched barren plat of Ground. But what need we to feek external Caufes in a Death which brought along fuch violent ones with it, a Cardinal of *Richelieu,* who was one of the beft Tempers and Conftitu-tions in the world, did fall under the burthen of the Anxieties and Agitations of the Mind. The fcabbard (as the Proverb faith) being worn out by the fharpnefs of the blade, muft of neceffity finde a vent : And how could it otherwife chufe; that a Man who for the fpace of ten or twelve years together had oppofed himfelf to all the Injuries both of Time and of War, fhould not at length fall under the activenefs of a foul which feldom gave him any reft, which govern-ed and directed the Reins of three reftive King-doms, unaccuftomed to the noble and famous Trappings of a Military Government; and who moreover was to direct and guide the Confci-ences as well as the Bodies of Men, and their Reafons as well as their Wills. It had not been confiderable had the Intereft of *England* onely required that his Cares had been limitted wit hin the Pales which the Sea prefcribes to her Pre-cincts; But as the caufe of the Difeafe was from abroad,

abroad, and that from the Closets of the Escurial, the Spaniards had imployed their false Piety as well as their *Peru* Gold, to discover and molest the repose of *England*; so fire and flame was to be applied without, and it was necessary to penetrate into the very secret causes of the evils. The People of the Cities of the Continent were to be disabused, and the Soldiery were to be overcome in open field. The Mines of *Mexico* were to be looked into, and the extent of that Ambition was to be curtailed, which boasts it self both to see the Sun set and rise.

These were vast imployments indeed of a large activity, to run through these undertakings, the fervor of them was scorching; and although the Heavens did second these lawful Designes withall its Graces, yet it could not without a Miracle, and without destroying the secondary Causes, hinder the separation of a Soul from a Body which it had so often employed, and so efficaciously seconded the grand Affairs both of State and War for the Peace, Glory, and Tranquillity of three Nations. Wherefore Nature it self did witness her grief some two or three dayes before, by an extraordinary Tempest and violent gust of weather; insomuch that it might have been supposed, that her self had been ready to dissolve; or that the Masterpiece of Nature suffered a violent agitation. And as the Death of the Sun of Righteousness was foretold by an Eclipse of the Sun, which covered the surface of the whole Earth with Darkness: In like manner, at the death of the

People

People of *England's Hercules*, both Force and Nature were let loose to shake the very Elements; and by the reuniting of their violence, like unto those who are ready to give up the Ghost, to leave some marks of an extream dissolution; all which is so lively set forth by the quaintest Wit of these times, as that I shall not inlarge any further upon this observation, but shall onely content my self to repeat unto you his Verses, who expresseth it more elegantly and copiously then my rough Prose can possibly reach to. *Mr. E. Waller.*

Upon the late Storm, and his Highness death ensuing the same.

We must resign, Heaven his great soul doth claim,
In Storms as loud as his immortal fame.
His dying groans, his last breath shakes our Isle,
And Trees uncut fall for his Funeral Pile;
About his Palace there broad roots were tost,
Into the Air, so Romulus was lost.
New Rome in such a tempest mist their King,
And from obeying fell to worshipping.
On Ætna's top, thus Hercules lay dead,
With ruin'd Oaks and Pines about him spread;
Those his last fury from the Mountain rent,
Our dying Hero from the continent.
Ravish whole Towns and Forts from Spaniards
As his last Legacy to Brittain left.   (refr,
The Ocean which so long our hopes confin'd
Could give no limits to his vaster minde:
Our bounds inlargement was his latest toil,

Nor

Nor hath he left us Prisoners to our Isle.
Under the Tropick is our Language spoke,
And port of Flanders *hath receiv'd our Yoke,*
From Civil Broyls he did us disingage,
Found nobler objects for our Martial rage;
And with wise conduct to his Countrey shew'd,
Their ancient way of conquering abroad.
Ungrateful then it were no tears allow,
To him that gave us peace and Empire too :
Princes that fear'd him grieve concern'd to see,
No pitch of glory from the Grave is free.
Nature her self took notice of his death,
And sighing swell'd the Sea with such a breath ;
That to remotest shores her billows rould,
The approaching fate of their Great Ruler *told.*

And truly I had need of all *Parnassus* his art
to sweeten and mollifie the bitterness of this
death, which causeth my pen to fall to the
ground, and would cast up my Muse into a pitti-
ful swound, did not all the rest of the Muses
come to her aid, and sprinkle her with some of
that divine Water which nourisheth her, to
make her revive again, and to restore her to her
strength, to announce to posterity the time,
the day, and the manner when and how his late
Highness our great *Oliver* breathed his last.

After his late Highness had therefore been
sick about a fortnight of a Disease which at the
beginning was but an Ague, on a Friday being
the third of *September* 1658. in the Morning, he
gave all the signs of a dying person, and for
whom the Physicians had onely Vows and Prayers

ers in reserve : However, he remained in that manner till about three of the Clock in the afternoon, when as his Soul which had alwayes retained the upper hand of his Body, preserved her Empire till the last moment ; he had alwayes his wits about him, and his perfect and intire understanding, and continued to deliver those Oracles which were necessary to establish, after so great a loss, the Peace and Tranquility of *England* ; and immediately to repair the ruines which so dangerous a dissolution had threatned the State withall, and might cause in the mindes of every particular person.

His greatest and most important care was to name a *Protector* to be his successor, which he did with Reasons so little favouring of his own interests and worldly concernments, as that he testified, that being not content to have sacrificed himself for the common good by the shortning of his dayes, he was willing to consecrate his Children thereunto, by the lading of them with the heavy burden of those weighty mysteries, which may well be termed a Royal and Gilt Servitude.

Which succession was so necessary to the Peace and Tranquility of the State, that the Commonwealth and the Elective Kingdoms are constrained to imitate it ; and the successive Monarchies have oftentimes done more with a yong Prince in a Cradle, hung betwixt two Trees in the midst of their Camp, then they would have done by the Orders and the Examples of the most expert Captains : But when as the Age,

R   Ex-

Experience, and Deferts of a Son do unite and combine in the Love and Memory of the vertues of a Father, what fhall not betide fo wife and worthy a choice ? and what fhall not be thence expected? For who can with more reafon hope to be feared, loved, and obeyed by a whole Nation, fave the worthy Heir of him, who hath rendred them fo formidable, and who hath ruled over, and governed them fo tenderly and meekly? How fhould unavoidable and ftrange changes have been prevented, if domeftick broils had not been fhunned? and whom could we thave better met with the refemblance of a Father, who never had his equal in Prudence, Fortune, and Valour, fave in a Son ?

Politicians and Nature delight in the diverfifying of their works; the one produceth few men alike, and the other delights in the condemning and deftroying of the defigns of thofe who have preceded them, to the end, that they may thereby fhew their own good parts, and rather appear Originals then Copies. After the giving of thefe and like Orders, and the fettling of the moft important Concernments of the State, this great Perfonage gave up the Ghoft, juft like a man that falls afleep through the toil of a laborious task. The enfuing night was ferene and peaceful, like unto thofe who difplay their Sable Veil fpangled with Stars, to deck and wrap up the Sun after its long and ferious ardent Courfe.

He died in the midft of his Victories and Triumphs, after he had caufed all the fair fruits which

which shall be reaped for ever by *England*, as well in the Continent, as within the Circumference of its Isles, to bud forth into Blossoms and Flowers. He dyed in a Bed of Bucklers, and on a Pillow of Caskets, and though the Wreaths of the Imperial *Laurel* which invironed his head did wither at the Groans of his Agony, it was onely to make place for a richer Diadem which was prepared for him in Heaven; and which must needs be more sumptuous and resplendent, in that it is ingrafted upon that Christian humility wherewith he did so constantly refuse a temporal Crown, which was due unto his deserts, and which was profered him several times by the People of *England*: and although he be dead, yet he is living, nay, triumphing, and pronouncing Oracles to his very last Groans, most clear and intellegible Oracles; and as being inspired by the Spirit of the God of Truth, he dyed like a second *Vespasian*, who even on his Death-bed continued to enlarge the Bounds of his Empire, and as long as he had breath, ceased not to dispatch several Businesses of consequence; answering the Physicians who reproved him, as the Emperour did, *That an Emperour ought to dye standing*. Truly it is a great comfort at the Article of death, to dye profitably for Heaven, and for the good of ones Countrey.

But before we close his Eyes, let us once more reflect on the constancy wherewith he expects her last assaults, and with how much fear and trembling this inexorable one sets upon him unarmed, and resolved to yield to her; and however she was accustomed to cast her darts before him, yet she is afraid, she trembles and hides her treacherous sythe, and never producing it till she sees her blow sure. How oftentimes approaching him in the heat of Battels, armed with despair and horrour, was she constrained to turn her back, and to serve him for an Instrument of Victory, whom she was resolved to have laid along? How often hath she been seen to change colour, and to embrace the weaker party, to the end she might shew her force, and cut down a greater number of victimes? Self-Interest is then made this insensible one grieve for those which she had rashly slain on *Olivers* side, she lost by their not being, since her sacrifices were there lessened, and that *Olivers* Arm alone was forced often to supply the absence of his companions, or their ill fortunes. But as the love of this step-dame was false, so likewise was it converted into rage as soon as his late Highness caused Peace to succeed War, and that he outvied this furious Hag by the undaunted courage; as then she brake off all intelligence with force and horrour, and she raised up from Hell all the malicious and subtil Furies, both Envy and Treason came to her relief and aid; and by a sacrilegious Spell, she hath sought the Blood of Christ in the very Sacrament thereof to compose her Poyson; and by abominable witchcrafts she sowed sedition in the Hearts of the People; she bewitched the Wise, she blinded the Nobles, and finally she therewith coloured

ed

ed and cloaked all her moſt black and horrid
Deſigns. But on *Oliver* his late Higneſs, ſhe
could never faſten her baits, finding him alwayes
armed with that Antidote which he renewed
daily on the ſame Altars whence ſhe ſucked her
venom. He alwayes oppoſed his Wiſdom to her
Craft, his Juſtice to her Violence, his Prayers to
her Impieties, and his Clemency to her Obſti-
nacy. The Tempeſt invironed him on all ſides,
but he was in the Ark; his Enemies ſet upon
him whileſt he was aſleep, but the Character of
God which was imprinted in his Forehead, cauſed the Sword to fall out of their hands; and
Goliah with his Legions of Philiſtines fell down
at the ſole report of his Sling.

Finally, God hath made him to paſs ſafe
through the lifted up Waves of his Enemies, in
which themſelves were drowned; and in caſe
the Sea did prove Red, God be praiſed it was
not by his Blood, nor by the ſtains of his Soul
which abhorred all kinde of Cruelty. For if the
Pardons which he granted were put in an equal
balance with the Deaths which happened during
the time wherein his Power was as yet but limitted, it would be found, that he did not alwayes
give ear to the prudent Politician, to abandon
himſelf from the meekneſs and generoſity of his
natural inclinations. Thoſe who ſhall read the
Hiſtories of ſuch like Revolutions as theſe, will
finde that they never attained to ſo high a pitch
of Grandor, by ſuch meek and merciful means,
and ſo void of paſſion. Wherefore his peaceable and natural Death hath been alſo a Reward

R 3 for

for his so great a Moderation ; nor can any one
doubt but Heaven hath had a particular care
of that life, which hath been so often attempted
and so desperately assaulted : Not but that he
would happily have rather chosen to have dyed
with his Sword in his hand, for the Glory of
God and the Defence of his Countrey, as better
befitting his Warlike humor and Men of Courage, but Heaven had otherwise evidenced its Miracles in his preservation.   Nor had our Champion had the glory to have wrestled with this
powerful Enemy upon unequal terms, *and in an*
estate wherein the imbecillity of the Spirit hath
no other relief but that of Grace and Reason :
This his preservation was also an effect of his
Prayers, which he had chosen with a great deal
of prudence out of the holy Writs.   He caused
one of his Gentlemen often to read the tenth
Chapter of *Matthew's* Gospel ; and twice a day
himself rehearsed the 71. *Psalm* of *David*, which
hath so near a relation to his Fortune and to his
Affairs, as that one would believe it had been a
Prophesie purposely dictated by the holy Ghost
for him ; or else that this great Personage was a
Mortal Figure of that great Favourite of God,
who hath done so many marvellous things with
such slender beginnings , passing through so
many obstacles, difficulties, and dangers : so likewise was it very just , that he should enter into
the eternal Rest on the like day wherein he had
undergone such great and glorious Labours and
Dangers ; and that he should triumph over
Death even in his weakness , at the like time
wherein

wherein he had overcome her at her fulleſt ſtrength and greateſt advantages. This conformity happened unto him as well as to ſeveral other great Perſonages of the Earth, but by ſuch obſervable and reiterated notable actions, as that it is void of all doubt but the Heavens had foretold by the Stars (which are the Looking-glaſſes and Rule of all famous Mens Lives) the Events of our glorious Protectors ſucceſſes. To inſtance in ſome, *Alexander* the Great was born on the ſixth day of *April*, on the like day the famous Temple of *Diana* at *Epheſus* was burnt, preſaging that fire which this Conqueror ſhould kindle in *Aſia*. On a ſixth day of *April* he overcame *Darius* King of *Perſia* in a Battle; and on the like day he departed this life: whereunto there may be added, that his Birth was preceded by a famous Victory which the Greeks his Subjects obtained on a ſixth day of *April* againſt the Perſians hard by *Plutea*, and by a Naval Combat which alſo happened the ſame day. So likewiſe *Pompey* was born and triumphed on a like day, to wit, the thirtieth of the Moneth of *September*. *Charles* the Fifth the Emperour had alſo ſuch like obſervable Encounters: he was born on a twenty fourth of *February*, and being twenty four years old, on the like day he obtained a great Victory, in which a great King was taken priſoner. And on a twenty fourth day of *February*, he was crowned Emperour by the Pope.

But not to look any further then our own Countrey, and into our own Hiſtories; It is ob-

ſerved

served that his late Highness our present Lord Protector, *Richard*, was Installed in his Protectorship on the like day, being a third day of *September*, when as *Richard* the First, that Famous King of *England*, so much spoken of in the Histories by reason of his great Wit, Understanding, and Resolution, began his Reign; an accident which cannot choose but promise a most favourable Omen and good Token. In like manner his late Highness had more favourable and famous dayes encountring together, then any of those foregoing Worthies which we have specified.

For on a third of *September* he was confirmed in his Protectorship by the Parliament. On a third of *September* he gained in *Scotland* that famous Battel of *Dunbar*. On a third of *September* he gained that great Battel at *Worcester*. And Finally, on a third of *September* his glorious life was Crowned with a peaceable and resolved death in the midst of all his Triumphs; in his Palace at *White-hall*, with all the comforts which good hopes could give in his posterity, both to his Children, and to the Companions of his Fortune.

The Corps of his late Highness having been Embalmed and wrapped up in a sheet of Lead, was on the six and twentieth of *September*, about ten of the Clock at night, privately removed from *White-hall* to *Sommerset-house*, being onely attended by his own Domestick Officers and Servants, as the Lord Chamberlain, and Comptroller of the Houshold, the Gentlemen of the Life-guard, the Guard of Halberdiers, and divers

vers

vers other Officers and Servants, two Heralds of Arms went next before the Corps, which was placed in a morning Hearse, drawn by six Horses; in which manner it was carried to *Sommerset-House*, where it remained for some dayes in private untill things were in a readiness to expose it in State to a publick view, which was performed with the following order and Solemnity.

The first Room at *Sommerset-House* where the Spectators entred, was formerly the Presence Chamber, compleatly hung with Black, at the upper end whereof was placed a Cloth of State with a Chair of State under the same.

The manner of his Highness lying in State.

The second large Room was formerly the Privy Chamber, hung with Black, with a Cloth and Chair of State under the same.

The third Room was formerly the Withdrawing Room, hung with Black Cloth, & had a Cloth and Chair of State in it as the former; all which three large Rooms were compleatly furnished with Scutcheons of his Highness Arms crowned with the Imperial Crown; and at the head of each Cloth of State was fixed a large majestique Scutcheon fairly painted and gilt upon Taffity.

The fourth Room where both the Corps and the Effigies did lye, was compleatly hung with Black Velvet, and the Roof was cieled with Velvet, and a large Canopy or Cloth of State of black Velvet fringed, was plated over the Effigies made to the life in Wax. The Effigies it self being apparel'd in a rich suit of uncut Velvet, robed in a little Robe of Purple Velvet, laced with a rich Gold Lace, and furr'd with Ermins;

upon

upon the Kirtle was the Royal large Robe of
the like purple Velvet, laced and furred with Ermins; with rich strings and tassels of Gold,
the Kirtle being girt with a rich embroidered
Belt, wherein was a fair Sword, richly gilt and
hatch'd with Gold, hanging by the side of the
Effigies. In the right hand was the Golden Scepter, representing Government; in the left
hand the Globe, denoting Principality; upon
the Head a purple Velvet Cap furr'd with Ermins, signifying Regality: Behinde the Head
there was placed a rich Chair of State of tissued
Gold, and upon the Cushion which lay thereon
was placed an Imperial Crown set with precious
Stones. The Body of the Effigies lay upon a
Bed of State covered with a large Pall of black
Velvet, under which there was spread a *fine*
Holland Sheet upon six stools of tissued Cloth
of Gold: on the sides of the Bed of State was
placed a rich suit of compleat Armour, representing his late Highness Command as General;
at the Feet of the Effigies stood *his Crest* according to the custom of ancient Monuments.

The Bed of State whereupon the Effigies did
thus lie, was ascended unto by two steps covered with the aforesaid Pall of Velvet, the whole
work being compassed about with Rails and Bal-
lasters covered with Velvet; at each corner
whereof there was placed an upright Pillar covered with Velvet, upon the tops whereof were
the four Supporters of the Imperial Arms, bearing Banners or Streamers Crowned. The Pillars
were adorned with Trophies of Military Honour
carved

carved and gilt, the pedeſtalls of the Pillars had Shields and Crowns gilt which compleated the whole work. Within the Rails and Ballaſters ſtood eight great Silver Candleſticks, or Standarts, almoſt five foot high, with Virgin-wax Tapers of three foot long; next unto the Candleſticks there were ſet upright in Sockets the four great Standards of his Higneſs Arms, the Guydons, great Banners, and Banrolls of war being all of Taffity very richly gilt and painted. The Cloth of State which covered the Bed of State, and the Effigies, had a Majeſtick Scutcheon; and the whole Room was fully and compleatly adorned with Taffity Scutcheons: ſeveral of his late Highneſs's Gentlemen attending bare-headed round about the Bed of State in Mourning; and other of his Highneſs's Servants waiting in the other Rooms, to give directions to the ſpectators, and to prevent diſorders.

After which, his late Highneſs Effigies was ſeveral dayes ſhown in another Room, ſtanding upon an Aſcent under a rich Cloth of State; veſted in royal Robes having a Scepter in one hand, and a Globe in the other, a Crown on his Head, his Armour lying by him at a diſtance, and the Banners, Banrolls, and Standards being placed round about him, together with the other Enſigns of Honour: the whole Room which was ſpacious being adorned in a majeſtical manner, and ſeveral of his late Highneſs's Gentlemen attending about the Effigies bare-headed, in which manner the Effigies continued until the ſolemnization of the Funerals.

His late Highneſs ſtanding in State.

On

On the three and twentieth day of *November* in the morning, the time appointed for the solemnization of the Funerals of his late Highness, the several persons of Honour and quality which were invited to attend the Interment, being come to *Somerset-house,* and all things being in a readiness to proceed; the Effigies of his late Highness standing under a rich Cloath of State in the manner afore specified, was first shown to the company, and afterwards removed and placed on a Hearse richly adorned and set forth with Scutcheons and other Ornaments; the Effigies it self being vested in Royal Robes, a Scepter in one hand, a Globe in the other, and a Crown on the Head: after it had been a while thus placed in the middle of a Room, it was carried on the Hearse by ten of his late Highness Gentlemen into the Court-yard, where a very rich Canopy of State was born over it by six other of his late Highness Gentlemen till it was brought and placed on the Chariot, at each end whereof was a seat wherein sate two of his late Highness's Gentlemen of the Bed-Chamber, the one at the Head and the other at the Feet of the Effigies. The Pall which was made of Velvet and the white linnen was very large, extending on each side of the carriage and was born up by several persons of Honour thereunto appointed. The Chariot wherein the Effigies was conveyed, was covered with black Velvet, adorned with Plumes and Scutcheons, and was drawn by six Horses covered with black Velvet, and each of them adorned with black Plumes of Feathers.

From

From *Somerset-house* to *Westminster* the streets were railed in, and strawed with Sand ; the Soldiers being placed on each side of the steeets without the Rails, and their Ensigns wrapped up in a Cypress mourning Veil.

The manner of the proceeding to the Interment,
was briefly thus.

First, a Knight Martial advanced on Horseback with his black Truncheon tipt at both ends with Gold, attended by his Deputy and thirteen men on Horseback, to clear the way.

After him followed the Poor men of *Westminster* in mourning Gowns and Hoods, marching two and two.

Next unto them followed the Servants of the several persons of all qualities , which attended the Funeral.

These were followed by all his late Highness's Servants , as well inferiour as superiour, both within and without the Household, as also all his Highness's Barge-men and Water-men.

Next unto these followed the Servants and Officers belonging to the Lord Major and Sheriffs of the City of *London*.

Then came several Gentlemen and attendants on the respective Ambassadors , and the other Publique Ministers.

After those came the poor Knights of *Windsor* in Gowns and Hoods.

Then followed the Clerks, Secretaries , and other Officers belonging to the Army, the Admiralty

The several distinctions observed in the Funeral Solemnities.

miralty, the Treasury, the Navy, and Exchequer.

After these came the Officers in Command in the Fleet, as also the Officers of the Army.

Next followed the Commissioners for Excize, those of the Army, and the Committee of the Navy.

Then followed the Commissioners for the Approbation of Preachers.

Then came the Officers, Messengers, and Clerks belonging to the Privy Councel, and the Clerks of both Houses of Parliament.

Next followed his late Highness Physicians.

The Head Officers of the Army.

The Chief Officers and Aldermen of the City of *London.*

The Masters of the Chancery, with his Highness learned Councel at Law.

The Judges of the Admiralty, the Masters of Request, with the Judges in *Wales.*

The Barons of the Exchequer, the Judges of both Benches, and the Lord Major of *London.*

Next to these the persons allied in Blood to his late Hignes, and the Members of the Lords House.

After them the Publique Ministers of Forreign States and Princes.

Then the *Holland* Ambassador alone, whose Train was born up by four Gentlemen.

Next to him the *Portugal* Ambassador alone, whose Train was held up by four Knight of the Order of Christ.

And thirdly the *French* Ambassador, whose Train was also held up by four persons of quality
                                                    Then

Then followed the Lords Commiſſioners of the great Seal.

The Lords Commiſſioners of the Treaſury.

The Lords of his late Highneſs moſt Honorable Privy Councel.

After whom followed the chief Mourner, and thoſe perſons of quality which were his Aſſiſtants, and bare up his Train. All the Nobles were in cloſe Mourning, the reſt were but in ordinary, being diſpoſed in their paſſage into ſeveral Diviſions, being diſtinguiſhed by Drums and Trumpets, and by a Standard or Banner born by a Perſon of Honor and his aſſiſtant, and a Horſe of State covered with black Velvet, and led by a perſon of Honor, followed by two Grooms: Of which Horſes there were eleven in all, four covered with black Cloth, and ſeven with Velvet. Theſe being all paſſed in order, at length the Chariot followed with the Effigies, on each ſide of which were born ſix Banner Rolls, twelve in all, by as many perſons of Honor. The ſeveral pieces of his late Highneſs Armor were born by eight Honorable perſons, Officers of the Army, attended by a Herald and a Gentleman on each ſide. Next followed *Garter* principal King of Arms, attended with a Gentleman on each ſide bare-headed.

Then came the chief Mourner together with thoſe Lords and noble perſonages that were ſupporters and aſſiſtants to the chief Mourner.

Then followed the Horſe of Honor in very rich Trappings embroidered upon Crimſon Velvet, and adorned with white, red, and yellow
Plumes

Plumes, and was led by the Master of the Horse.

Finally, in the close of all followed his late Highness Guard of Halberdiers, and the Warders of the Tower.

The Solemnity was mannaged with a great deal of State from *Somerset-House* to *Westminster*, many thousands of people being Spectators in the Windows and upon the Scaffolds all along the way as it passed.

At the West Gate of the Abbey Church, the Hearse with the Effigies thereon was taken off again from the Chariot by those ten Gentlemen who placed it thereon before, and *in their passing* on to carry it into the Church, the Canopy of State was by the former six Gentlemen *born* over it again : In which stately manner it *was* carried up to the East end of the Abbey, *and* there placed in that Magnificent structure which was purposely erected there to receive it ; where it is to remain for some time exposed to publick view. The Corps having been some *dayes* before Interred in *Henry* the Seventh's *Chappel in* a Vault purposely prepared for the same, over which a costly Monument is preparing.

Thus have you a brief Relation of the last Ceremonies of Honor which were performed to the Memory of his late Highness, who by his Heroick Acts had so well deserved, as that my dull pen not able to express them, I shall remit the Reader to censure my endeavours, and submit to those that shall hereafter undertake to present the World with a larger Chronicle.

F I N I S.

THE
CHARACTER

of his late Serene Highness,

OLIVER,

Late Lord Protector:

With several Reflections on the foregoing History.

Seeing Philosophers are of opinion, that the Resemblance of Children to their Parents, as well in their bodily shapes and features, as in the Inclinations of their Souls, is produced by one and the self-same Cause; chiefly grounded upon this reason, That the one is the Representative of the other. And seeing moreover, that we may not attribute unto a material Cause an immaterial Effect, such as are all the operations of a Rational Soul, they reject the power of a forming vertue, the the Imaginary one, the Constellation of the Planets, and the qualities of the Seed. To fix

S

upon

upon a more sublime mystery, whereby God
would have the Legitimateness of Children and
Nephews to be manifested, rather by the better part of man, which is the Soul, then by his
Complexion, his Behaviour, his Speech, and
the shape of his Body. And that such glorious souls as are wrapt up as it were in
the body, should like unto a transparent sun
penetrate through those thick clouds, and by
that resplendency which they infuse through
the whole body, should attract the esteem and
veneration which they beget in men, either in
the Vulgar sort, who are onely taken with the
out-side, or in the malicious and envious, who
endeavour to smother those Talents in others
which they do not possess themselves.

Which truth, that we may the better make
good, it will not be amiss, having first represented unto you some of his late Highness the
Lord Protectors memorable Acts, to demonstrate unto you the greatness of his soul, and
how well it was placed, whereby all its
Heroical vertues may, as through a Chri-
stal glass, appear unto the eyes of the whole
world.

In this wise all Hystoriographers have proceeded, not onely in their describing of the live
of Illustrious Personages, but also in subduing
of Cities and Towns, Fortresses, and places of
Consequence, which no sooner had received the
Conquerours yoke, but the Origine and Foundations were narrowly pried into, the manner of
their being fortified was described, the form of
their

their being besieged, the assaults which they suffeined, and the glory which they acquired even by their surrendry upon honorable terms; whereas on the contrary, inconsiderate ones are quite neglected, their appellations and reductions being scarce deemed worthy to be specified in a History.

In like manner, since death after several vain attempts and successless assaults hath at length bereaved us of our Illustrious late Lord Protector, we shall give you the *Character* of his person, to let you see how much he resembled his glorious predecessors. And howbeit we may thereby somewhat diminish and detract from his glory, however so beautiful a soul as his was, accompanied by a body participating of all those Organs which were susceptible of such high and admirable operations, could not choose but produce the ensuing glorious effects?

In his person he somewhat exceeded the usual middle stature, but was well proportioned accordingly, being of a becoming fatness, well shaped, having a masculine face, a sparkling eye, both courteous and harsh at once, according as there was occasion; hardy and fierce in combats and reprehensions, tempered in counsels and meek, promising to the afflicted and suitors. He was of a strong constitution, and of an active body well disposed; an enemy both to ease and excess; and although in his youth he was capable of, yet he used not those fair and bewitching pleasures which a countrey (where idleness and wantonness did reign) doth afford to vigorous

con-

conftitutions with a great deal of mediocrity: in the War, he was active, vigilant, and circumfpect; and although he was doubtlefs one of the beft head-pieces in the world, yet he difdained not to conferre and take counfel with others, even in Affairs of the leaft concernment.

His greateft delight was to read men rather then books; and his Eloquence which was both Mafculine and Martial, was rather a natural gift then an effect of art, wherein he alwayes mingled fome paffages of the holyWrit, in which his piety had amply inftructed him; to which moft charming part as well as to his Sword, *he owed* moft of his Conquefts and Victories; being alwayes accuftomed to exhort and animate his Souldiers at the undertaking of any great enterprize, and before the giving of a battle; fo likewife after he had gained the victory, he himfelf did exprefs unto God his thankfulnefs and acknowledgements with fo profound an humility, as that he attributed unto God alone all his good fuccefs; and did conftantly refufe *all thofe* triumphs which were prepared for, and profered to his valour. He had an efpecial care to have Piety and Godlinefs reign in his Armies, and punifhed as a moft enormious crime, thofe who took Gods name in vain. Moreover, he loved his Souldiers as his Children, and his greateft care was to fee them provided for with all neceffaries requifite; by which forefight and providence, he was the better able to execute that fevere punifhment which he ufually caufed to be inflicted on thofe who plundred and fpoiled
the

the Peasants, for which crime he would not have pardoned his own brother, and on the other side he was alwayes most bountiful and liberal to his Souldiers, and those Pensions which are yet payed daily unto the old Souldiers, unto their Widows, and to the maimed and hurt men, may save those charges, which some Princes have been at to hire persons to weep and lament at their Funerals, and over their Tombs.

He took great delight to discourse of the Affairs of the World, and his own judgement did furnish him with such exact resolutions concerning the Government of his Estates, and touching the interests of other Princes, as without the entring into their Cabinets, or partaking of their Counsels, he discoursed very pertinently of their Affairs, and foretold their several issues and events. He likewise was an excellent Phisiognomer, and having once seriously considered any one, he was seldome deceived in the opinion he conceived of him. See History and Policy reviewed.

He married into the ancient and noble family of the *Blurchers*, whence the Earls of *Essex* were descended; his marriage bed was blessed with many Children, none of which did ever degenerate from the eminent vertues of their most Illustrious Father. His eldest son named *Richard* hath succeeded him in the Protectorship; his younger son named *Henry*, being at this time Lord Lieutenant of *Ireland*; both of them capable to follow their Fathers glorious footsteps, and to perfect and crown such hopeful, promising, though difficult, beginnings; their Father having as it were divided, shared,

and

and bestow inheritance into their youth (swelling with marvellous hopes) that most exquisite Quintessence of two great Talents, which he had acquired by his age and by his experience, so that the one of his sons may be stiled the *Jupiter*, and the other the *Mars of England*.

He had four Daughters, all of them Ladies of most eminent and vertuous disposition. The Lady *Bridget* first married unto the Lord *Ireton*, in his life time Lord Deputy of *Ireland*, a Personage of sublime worth, and afterwards espoused unto the Lord *Fleetwood*, sometimes Lord Deputy of *Ireland*, and at present Lieutenant General of all his Highness Forces. The Lady *Elizabeth* his second Daughter, married unto the Lord *Claypoll*, and dyed a little before her Father, of whom we shall speak hereafter. The third, the Lady *Mary*, espoused unto the Lord Viscount *Fauconberge*. And the youngest, the Lady *Frances*, her present widow, of the Lord *Robert Rich*, Grandchild to the late Earl of *Warwick*.

Nor did the change of his late Highness Fortunes in the least diminish or diminish the tenderness and affection which he ever bare towards the worthy Mother of so numerous and hopeful issue, and the absolute power which he had over all his Dominions, never gave him the least desire to captivate any heart, save that which God had given him in marriage. And that which is the most to be admired at, and seems to be the summe of all bliss, is, that the Almighty lent his late Highness so much life as to see all his Children disposed to the most gallant

fant perfonages, and allied to the moft Illuftrious Families of *England*, which are as fo many
props of his Fortune, and Fences againft the en-
viers of his Vertue.

He was an enemy to vain glorioufnefs & often-
tation, and although he was all as it were fire,
that is, of a paffionate conftitution; yet he had
fo overcome his paffions, that he was feldome or
never moved but when there was a great caufe
given: fo likewife was he more fubject to re-
prefs and keep in, then to give way to his paffion. The actions of his body denoted thofe of
his minde, his actions were in a manner without
motion, and without any forcings of the body;
in like manner his minde was not at all agitated,
nor his expreffions precipitated; fweetnefs and
tranquillity accompanied his thoughts and his
words; but when there was occafion to carry a
bufinefs, he expreffed himfelf with fo much vigour, as gave to underftand, that he was not eafily to be diffwaded from the thing he had once
refolved.

In like manner during the whole courfe of the
War, he never harboured the leaft thought of
changing of parties. And as for Ambition, which
is the onely paffion whereof envy it felf feems to
accufe him, the effects thereof were fo inconfide-
rable and unneceffary unto him, nay, fo unplea-
fing and unwelcome; and which is more, he fo
often refufed the pomps, delights, and gran-
dours which were profered him, that all the
world muft needs confefs, that where Nature
could claim fo fmall an intereft, the mafter and

directer

directer of Nature muſt needs have had a great
ſhare. Wherefore we may aver, with a great
deal of reaſon, That in caſe he hath hoorded
and laid up Treaſures, it hath been in the In-
trals of the Poor of all Sexes, and of all Nations,
of all Profeſſions and Religions, both at home
and abroad; inſomuch, that it hath been com-
puted, that out of his own private inſtinct particular Motions and pious Compaſſion, he di-
ſtributed at leaſt forty thouſand pounds a year
in Charitable Uſes, out of his own purſe, out of
ſuch Moneys as the Commonwealth did allow
him for his Domeſtique Expences, and for the
maintenance of his State, and the Dignity of
his Perſon, Family, and the keeping up the
ſplendour of his Court.

And the better to illuſtrate this matter, we
ſhall inſert an Eſſay of two examples of Generoſity and Gratitude, which are not to be parallel'd, ſave in the perſons of *Thomas* Lord *Cromwell,* his late Highneſs's predeceſſor, in *Henry*
the Eighth's Reign, and in the perſon of his late
Highneſs, *Oliver* Lord Protector.

An exam- In thoſe glorious dayes, when the Engliſh
ple of gra- young Gentry, endeavored to out-vie their
titude and elder Brothers, by undertaking far and dange-
generoſity rous journies into Forreign parts, to acquire
in the Lord glory by feats of Arms, and experiencing them-
Tho. Crom- ſelves in the Military Diſcipline; *Thomas
well.* *Cromwel* a younger Brother, to better his knowledge in Warlike Affairs paſſed into *France,*
and there trailed a Pike, accompanying the
French

French Forces into *Italy*, where they were defeated at *Gattellion*; whereupon our *English Voluntier* betook himself to *Florence*, designing to pass thence home again into *England*, but having lost all his equipage, and being in a necessitated condition, he was enforced to address himself to one *Signior Francisco Frescobald* an Italian Merchant, who corresponded at *London*; and making his case known unto him; *Frescobald* observing something remarkable, and a certain promising greatness in the Features, Actions, and Deportment of *Thomas Cromwel*, who gave an accoune of himself with so candid an ingenuity, and in such terms as beseemed his Birth, and the Profession he then was of, whereby he gained so much upon *Frescobald*, as (inviting him home to his house, he caused him to be accommodated with new Linnen and Clothes, and other sutable necessaries, kindly entertaining him, till such time as he testified a desire to return for *England*; when as to compleat his Generosity and Kindeness, he gave Mr. *Thomas Cromwel* a Horse, and sixteen Duccats in gold, to prosecute his journey homewards.

In process of time, several disasters and Bankrupts befalling *Signior Frescobald*, his Trading and Credit was not a little thereby impaired; and reflecting on the Moneys which were due unto him by his Correspondents in *England*, to the value of 15000. Duccats, he resolved to pass thither, and try whether he could happily procure payment.

During

During which interval of time, Mr. Thomas
Cromwell being a person endowed with a great
deal of Courage, of a transcendent Wit, hardy
in his undertakings, and a great Politician, had
by these his good qualities gotten himself entrance and credit at Court, and highly ingratia-
ted himself with King Henry the Eighth, having advanced himself to almost as high a pitch
of Honour, in as short a time, in a manner, as
his late Highness did not

The Lord Thomas Cromwell therefore riding
one day with a great Train of Noble Men towards the Kings Palace, chanced to espy on foot
in the streets Signior Frescobald, the Italian Merchant, in an ill plight; however, he immediately alighting from his Horse, embraced him before all the world, to the great astonishment of
the beholders; and chid him, that at his first
arrival he came not to visit him. Frescobald
being astonished at so unexpected an encounter,
and receiving so signal a favour from a personage
he could not call to mind he had ever known,
was quite surprized; and my Lord Cromwell's
pressing affairs at Court but permitting him the
while to acquaint him further who he was, onely engaged him to come and dine with him that
day, as Frescobald full of amazement, enquired
of the attendants who that great personage
might be? And hearing his name, he began to
call the Feature of his Face, and the Air of his
Person to mind; and so by degrees conceiving
with himself it might happily be the said Mr.
Thomas Cromwell whom he had back pursued at
Florence;

Florence; he enquired out his Lordships habitation, and attended his coming at Noon-tide, walking in his Court-yard. No sooner was the Lord *Thomas Cromwel* entred the same, (attended by several persons of quality, and officers of the Crown) but speedily alighting from his Horse, he embraced his friend *Frescobald* in the same manner he had done in the morning; and perceiving that the Lords which accompanied him were amazed at such a disproportioned familiarity, he told them that he was more obliged to *Frescobald* then to all the men in the world; owing unto him the making of his Fortune; and so proceeded to relate unto them the whole story which had befallen him at *Florence*. So great a delight do generous mindes take to account their foregoing Misfortunes, when their Grandor hath elevated them to such a pitch, as that they triumph over Shame, and are incapable of Ingratitude.

Frescobald was treated at Dinner with all the tenderness he could expect from so great a personage, and so good a friend; after which being carried up by the Lord *Cromwel* into his Closet, he was there presented with four bags of Gold, each containing four hundred Ducats, in return of his former civilities; which *Frescobald* (being of a gallant spirit) at first refused, but after several contestations was constrained to accept as an acknowledgement from the Lord *Cromwel*; who, moreover enquiring of him concerning his coming over, and affairs in *England*, and understanding his Losses, and that there

there were Moneys due to him, caused him to write down his Debters names; and by his Secretary summoned the several Merchants which were indebted to *Frescobald* (upon pain of his displeasure) to clear their Accounts with him, and to pay him within the space of fifteen days; which was accordingly performed: onely *Frescobald* freely forgave them the Use.

Over and above all which, the Lord *Thomas Cromwell* endeavoured to perswade his friend *Frescobald* to have remained in *England* the rest of his Dayes, profering to lend him a stock of 60000. Duccats to trade withall: But *Frescobald* being over-charged with all those grand obligations which the Lord *Cromwell* had conferred on him; having by his Lordships Generosity acquired enough to keep him from being necessitated all his life time; and deeming that the trading in good Works was incomparably more sure and gainful then in the richest Wares and Merchandizes, being resolved to quit Trading, and to end the rest of his dayes peaceably and quietly, he obtained leave of the Lord *Thomas Cromwell* to depart towards his own Countrey, freighted with so great obligations as caused in him a generous shame.

But the Almighty doth not alwayes recompense the fruits of good Works here on Earth, often repaying the greatest with the least rewards; and Heaven delights in the exercising of its great Vertues, by the Vices which are thereunto opposite: and as the most noblest Creatures are the slowest in the attaining to

their

their perfections, so the Almighty doth not immediately cause those Fruits to ripen, which are sowed here below by Christian Charity.

Wherefore to return to the Lord *Thomas Cromwell*, who had made the Match between *Anne* of *Cleve* and King *Henry* the Eighth, you shall see how he was rewarded for his Generosity and good Services; for this Princess *Anne* of *Cleve*, conceiving a certain womanish Jealousie, she knew not why nor wherefore, against the Lord *Thomas Cromwell*, save onely that she apprehended he had too great a power and sway with the King, never left off solliciting and importuning of him, till he caus'd the Lord *Thomas Cromwell* to be beheaded; by which sad compliance, the King lost the best Supporter of his Crown, and the faithfullest of his Servants and Subjects. The Lord *Thomas Cromwell* dyed without Heir Males, leaving one onely Daughter, espoused to one Mr. *Williams* a Gentleman of *Glamorganshire*, of a good Family, who, as we have before said, inherited little of his Father, save his Vertues, besides what his own Deserts had procured him, and what he might promise himself by the Match with this Heiress the Lord *Thomas Cromwels* Daughter: (from whence our Lord Protectors are lineally descended) and who was the lively representative of her Father, and the very pourtraiture of his great soul, as the Lady *Cleypool* was of his late Highness the Lord Protector.

Now that you may know on what occasion the

The Lord Tho. Cromwels Seed, Destiny, and end.

How the
Name of
Williams
came to be
changed
into that of
Cromwell.

the Name of *Williams* came to be changed into that of *Cromwel*; it happened when as King *Henry* the Eighth was in the midst of his Splendor, Pomp, and Magnificence; wallowing in the pleasures of a sumptuous Entertainment at Court, Mr. *Williams* (who had been a retainer to the late Lord *Thomas Cromwell*) made his appearance before the King in deep Mourning, like a dark Cloud eclipsing the Sun at Noontide. The King casting his eye upon so unexpected and dismal an Object, (which seemed to reproach his rash fault) was surprized and offended, at the interrupting of his *Pleasures*, by *Williams* so unseasonable apparition, wherefore the King asked him how he durst appear at Court in that garb? whereunto *Williams* replied with a sad but assured countenance, That not onely himself, but the King and all the Court had reason to mourn for the loss of the greatest and faithfullest of his Subjects and Servants, whose Death himself might one day chance to regret, when he should stand in *need of his* Councels and Fidelity. But the King whose thoughts were at that time taken up with his Pastimes, wished *Williams* to be gone, and to get himself cured of his Frenetick Mallady.

Some while after troubles arising, and the King finding himself in a strait for want of so faithful a Minister of State as the late Lord *Thomas Cromwel* was, whose life he had so inconsiderately taken away, began to reflect on the loss he had sustained, and how requisite it was,

was, for Princes, and great Potentates, to retain near their Persons, Men of Knowledge, Worth and Fidelity, and calling to minde the action and discourse of *Williams*, conceiving that it could not proceed but from a great soul endowed with extraordinary vertues, and such a one as might be useful and serviceable to him, he sent for him up to Court, and commanding him to take the name of *Cromwel* upon himself, (unto whom he had testified so much Fidelity and Gratitude) he invested him with all the Offices and Charges the late Lord *Thomas Cromwel* enjoyed near his person, and re-instated him again in all his Goods and Lands which had been confiscated, so that the Lord *Williams* assisted in the Kings Councel, as his Father in Law the Lord *Thomas Cromwel* before had done.

From this Noble Lord *Williams, alias Cromwel*, and the Illustrious Daughter of the renowned Lord *Thomas Cromwel*; his late Highness and our present Lord Protector are linearly descended; In whom the Almighty hath raised up and ripened those generous vertues of their predecessors, and hath elevated and spread their branches as high, as their deep roots had taken profound and vigorous Foundations.

His late Highness descent.

So that to compleat our parallel, we may observe by the fruits of this Illustrious Stock from whence his late Highness is descended; whether they retained their accustomed Generosity and Clemency; which we will not go about to prove by the Military Acts, in which they have outvied their Predecessors; nor by their Politick

and

and prudent Government of the State, in which they have at least equalized them; but by their private and domestick actions, since the resemblance of Children to their Parents may be more observed by the Features of the Face, then by the course of their lives, which are subject to vary, either by the inconstancy of Fortune, or the Communication of other men.

An example of his late Highness gratitude.

To come therefore to his late Highness the Lord Protector, and signalize his gratitude; we shall instance in the person of one *Duret* a French attendant of his Highness during his General-ship, who served him with so much Fidelity and Zeal, as that he intrusted him with the managing and conduct of the greatest part of his domestick Affairs; always retaining him nigh his person, bearing so great an affection towards him, and reposing so entire a confidence in him, as during his late Highness's great sickness which he had in *Scotland*, (and whereof it was thought he would have dyed) he would not be served by any one, nor receive any nourishment, or any thing else that was administred unto him, save from the hands of *Duret*, who both day and night continued to watch by his Master; tending him with a special care and assiduity, not giving himself a Moments rest untill his late Highness had recovered his perfect health; which long and continual watches of *Duret*, and the pains he had taken in the administring unto his Master, plunged him into a sad fit of sickness; during which, this faithful servant received all the acknowledgements

ledgements which his good and zealous services had demerited, his late Highness applying all the possible cures he could, not onely by his commands, but by his personal visits, (so oft as his urgent Affairs would permit him) to comfort *Duret*, and to see all things applyed, that might conduce to his recovery: but *Durets* hour being come, he was content to lay down his life in his Masters service; and the Physicians having quite given him over, his late Highness would needs render him his last good offices, by comforting him at his death, by his sensibleness of his good services, and the extream zeal and affection he had born to his person; which although he could not requite unto him, yet his Highness assured him he would manifest his acknowledgements thereof unto his Parents and Kindred: Whereunto *Duret* replyed, That the honour he had received in having served so good and great a Master, and the glory he reaped in having laid down his life for the preservation of his Highness, and of so good and glorious a Cause, was extream satisfactory unto him in his death. That he had a Mother and a Sister, with some Kindred in *France*, who were unworthy his Highness thoughts, or reflecting on them; however that he remitted them to his Highness gracious consideration. And so *Duret*, his good and faithful servant breathed his last.

In which contract of grief, and resolution of acknowledgement, his late Highness may be said to have harboured the same thoughts as *Henry* the Eighth did; perswading himself that

T   he

he had been the Author of *Durets* death, though in a far innocenter way; However his late Highness retained all the resentments and sensibleness of the acknowledgements and gratitude, expressed by his generous predecessor the Lord *Thomas Cromwel*, towards his dear Friend *Frescobald*.

For his late Highness immediately sent over For *Durets* Mother, Sister, and two Nephews out of *France*, and would have the whole Family of the *Durets* to come and establish themselves here in *England*; that he might the better manifest his Love and Gratitude in their persons, towards his deceased faithful servant. And whereas by reason of the continuance of the Scotch Wars, his late Highness was at that time, as it were confined to the North, he wrote unto her Highness, the now Lady Protectoress Dowager, his wife, that she should receive and use *Durets* Mother, Sister, and Allies, accordingly as she praised the good offices of his deceased faithful servant, to whose cares, pains, and watchings he owed the preservation of his own life; and that she should proportion that kindness which during his absence she should show unto them, unto the love which she bore unto him; insomuch, that *Durets* Mother was by her Highness admitted into her own Family, and seated at her own Table; his Sister was placed in the rank and quality of a Maid of Honour to her Highness; and his two Nephews were admitted to be her Highnesses Pages; whereby the Almighty Crowned *Durets* good and faithful services towards his

Ma-

...ster, and his piety and observance towards his
...ther and Sister, whose onely support he was
his life time; with the rich Flowers of Pro-
...rity, and with the Fruits of Fortune, advan-
...g them as fast as the sad destiny did his pre-
...itated death.

And no sooner was his late Highness returned
...o *England* after the conquest of *Scotland*, and
...e glorious Victory he had obtained at *Worce-*
...r, full freighted with the resplendency of his
...ble atchievements; but he desired to see *Duret's*
...other, Sister, and Nephews, enquiring how
...ey had been received, and treated; and whe-
...er they were well pleased to be in *England*;
...d as soon as they appeared in his presence, he
...uld not retain his generous tears for the loss
...*Duret*; nor could he cease to testifie his in-
...ard grief for him, comforting the good old
...entlewoman Mrs. *Duret*, by the mouth of his
...hildren who spake French, telling her, *She had*
ot lost her son, although dead; for that himself
ould be her son, since the preservation of his life
ad its being from her entralls; that both her and
is Duret was with a better Master; a Master,
who was his Master also; and whose recompences
and rewards were far greater and more assured
then these worldly ones. And that the great
...houghts of his heart might not lose their force
...nd energy, by his imploying of anothers tongue
to expres them; this great Personage who never made use of the French language to enter-
tain the Ambassador of Kings and Princes withall, did put himself to the trouble of learning

T 2   some

some French words, with which he alwayes was used to chear up and comfort the good old Woman whensoever he met her : and he that was wont to swim in the blood of his enemies, and could look with an undiscomposed brow on thousands of men, and of his friends, lying dead on the Field after a battle, had so much tenderness for the loss of one of his domestique Servants, as that he could not refrain from tears when he beheld any of *Durets* relations. Nor need we to wonder hereat, since his late Highnesses general spirit contained as well private as publique Vertues. And his Reason which was alwayes mistress of his Passions, knew full well how to imploy them on such occasions, and at such times as they were most requisite and commendable : to let us see, That the Dignity of a General and a Protector, had not made him relinquish the quality of a Man ; and that Maximes and Reasons of State had forced several things from him, which were absolutely repugnant to his natural inclinations. Besides, this great Politician knew, that the greatest part of Famous Men, which Fortune had elevated to the top of her Wheel, were for the most part come to untimely ends by the corruption of their domestique Servants, or the treachery of their intimatest Friends and bosom Favourites : in regard whereof, his late Highness lamented the more the loss of this his Faithful Servant.

Nor need we to wonder hereat, since Fortune had heaped all the perfections of Vertues in his great Soul, which he evidently manifested,

by

By his so orderly, and peaceably re-uniting, and as it were, matching together the Vertues both of War and Peace; the ruffness and harshness of War, with the tenderness of Nature; their Licentiousness with Piety; Confusion with good Order; and so resplendent an eminent Greatness, to such inconsiderate, abject, and humble domestique considerations.

Wherefore this Nation may account it self thrice happy, in enjoying such sublime rising Powers to govern it, who are able to distinguish between Good and Evil; and who suffer not themselves to be puffed up so high, as that they scorn and disdain to look downwards, and so stand not in need (as the waters poured far from the Ocean) of a borrowed and corrosive salt, to preserve things from corruption.

Thus as I have already given you rather a Glimpse then a Character of his late Highness his Person, I shall now render you some other considerable Remarks of his Affairs.

After the discoveries of an hundred Plots and Designs laid open and frustrated, the defeating of many jealous parties all of them convinced; and finally, sundry Forreign Negotiations and Treaties, which hath given you occasion as well to admire his Judgement as his Valour, whence you have found as bold undertakings to have proceeded from his late Highness, as ever were commented; and as admirable Conquests on the Continent, as may well answer the ancient (though long time dormatick) Valour of the English Nation.

To confider how he joyned the Piety and good Order of *Numa* with the Vigour and Force of *Romulus*, in those foundations which he laid of this new and Warlike Empire; which although they scarce budded forth of the earth, are never the less substantial enough to bear up a solid building; and do sufficiently discover all the several beautiful Repartitions of the same in a most exquisite manner, and in a goodly ground plot.

First, his late Highness settled such a Military Discipline, as partaking of the Vertues of the three first Roman Founders, did strike a terrour into the most ambitious Monarchs of the earth, and doth give Instructions, or rather read Lectures on both the Christian and Moral Vertues unto that Nation which pretends to be the wisest and most Religious of all the world. I believe that if a Croysade had armed all the Priests and Religious Men, there would not be so strict an order observed in their Christian Military Discipline, as that which we now see is established in *England*, where Sobriety flourisheth amidst abundance, in a Countrey where formerly Debauchery was accounted as a Gallantry, and converted into a custom; where Modesty is wedded to Cruelty, Justice with the extremity of Power, Meekness with the stubborness of Arms, War with Piety, Valour with Fear and Obedience. And since we speak of the Piety of this English *Pompilius*, may we not say that the Goddess *Ageria* did nightly in his solitudes appear unto him.

See History and Policy reviewed.

Not

Nor need we to say that he made use of fire and flames by a barbarous and unchristian-like Zeal to establish the truth of the Gospel. Nor did he send millions of Pagans to Hell, thereby to be strong enough to force five hundred against their wills into Heaven: The Piety of this our Common Father was void of Envy and Cruelty. He hath defied the Tyrants over mens Consciences by Clemency and Charity, and hath caused those who profess those two Vertues before all others (which are more sublime though less profitable to our neighbours, and consequently of less concernment) to doubt, whether or no the Quality of the most *Christian King* is not far better then that of the *Catholique*. All which being maturely considered, we may say when a State erreth both in the Ecclesiastique and Politique Government, he that is invested with the Sovereign Power, far from being reputed a Tyrant, is accountable before God if he doth refuse the same, and if he lets that Talent remain useless which may otherwise be advantageous to the whole world.

To say more of his Generosity, this Vertue he highly recommended above all others unto his Ministers of State, and unto his Ambassadors, and unto his Children; and whereof that noble Lady *Cleypoll*, his Daughter of worthy memory, did give so many evidences during her life, and even at the Article of her Death, as that she thereby did beget tears in the most obstinate and hardiest enemies of this State. A worthy Daughter of so famous a Father; whom Heaven too

T 4   soon

foon fnatched away both from the Vertuous and from the Miferable, and whofe foul did admirably correfpond with her Fortune, and the Majefty of her Comportment. How many of the Royalift prifoners got fhe not freed? How many did fhe not fave from Death whom the Laws had condemned? How many perfecuted Chriftians hath fhe not fnatcht out of the hands of the tormenters, quite contrary unto that *Herodias* who could do any thing with her father. She imployed her Prayers even with Tears to fpare fuch men whofe ill fortune had defigned them to fuffer: when as this grand Heroe being tranfported as it were, and even ravifhed to fee his own Image fo lively defcribed in thofe lovely and charming Features of that winning Sex, could refufe her nothing; infomuch, that *when* his Clemency and Juftice did balance the pardon of a poor Criminal, this moft charming Advocate knew fo skilfully to difarm him, that his Sword falling out of his hands, his arms onely ferved to lift her up from thofe knees on which fhe had caft her felf, to wipe off her tears, and to imbrace her. So likewife it is believed, that this illuftrious Princefs precipitated death, did not a little contribute to his late Highneffes fickning; all whofe noble parts were found to be very found and whole, onely his Heart, which forrow had feized and dryed up. Nor did he long out-live her, fince it was impoffible he fhould furvive the love of fo generous a difpencer of his Clemency and Generofity.

For brevity, I fhall make choice of one of the
Am-

Ambaſſadours of this Commonwealth, to denote the ſplendor of the glorious Miniſters of this generous Prince; he being in ſuch a place where he hath more occaſion then any of the reſt, to give far ampler marks of the moſt Heroical Vertue, which acquires more glory to the victorious then the victory it ſelf, and which is the moſt aſſured Character of a true Chriſtian, his Excellency the Lord *Lockhart*, Ambaſſador in the Court of *France*, General of his Highneſs Forces in *Flanders*, and Governour of the Town of *Dunkirk*, who is eſpouſed to that moſt renowned Lady one of his late Highneſs's Neeces. In both which noble Perſonages we may behold at once ſhining forth thoſe two happy and glorious Talents, which moſt of all render perſons of their Birth and Quality recommendable and famous. His perſon ſeems onely to have been ſent into *France* to charm the whole Nation, and to attract and accumulate graces; and did he not expoſe himſelf to ſo many dangers and hazards in the Wars, men might eaſily believe that after he had long born Arms in *Holland*, in *France*, and ten years ſpace for the late King of *England*, that he onely ranged himſelf on the victorious ſides to ſave the Kings Party, and to reinſtate them in their Lands and Goods.

Wherefore the Generoſity, Courteſie, and Affability of his late Highneſs did ſo ſuperabound, as that no one perſon ever departed from his preſence unſatisfied; for he received the Petitions of all men, he heard their Grievances, and his charitable memory was ſo retentive, as that

that he never forgot their requests, but made it his chief object to bear them in minde, and most tenderly to provide for them. He esteemed those he had overcome, and took a delight to pardon them, and to make them sharers of his good Fortune ; provided that they would give over to make themselves unfortunate , by their obstinacy. He was used to say, that Hearts were as well to be overcome as Fortresses , and that the one were no more to be demolished then the other, because they had belonged to other Masters ; insomuch , that he esteemed it a great Conquest to have gained a gallant Man to his party. And as for those who have been put to death in his time , they may be said to have been their own Judges, and their own executioners. And however Politicians hold, *that* in the changing of a Government , all things ought likewise to be changed if possible , even the very Religion it self, (were men prophane enough to meddle therewith) and that Cruelty ought wholly to banish Clemency, *yet all men* know, that as to the point of Religion, he did leave things as he found them ; and that he *saved* more lives by thousands, then obstinacy and despair did cause to perish. Nay, he did even wish when he came to have a more absolute power towards the latter end of his dayes , that those which had been put to death were yet alive; protesting solemnly, that if he could not change their hearts he would have changed their Dooms, and convert their deaths into a banishment ; which is easily to be believed, by the

good-

goodness which he hath exercised towards the children of such as were put to death, even those who were his most implacable enemies; leaving them in possession both of their Goods and Titles; and whose losses he hath recompensed by such civillities as doth evidence, he learned not his Politicks in *Machiavils* School; who teacheth, that the children and all the Generation were to be exterminated together with their Fathers; so that many men wished that his Highnesse power had been as absolute ten years since as it was some years before his death.

So likewise those Alliances which he made, and those Wars which he undertook, had all of them motives of Generosity, and were founded on Equity and Reason; if so be we consider the very first whereinto he onely stept by the degree of a Captain, and which may be termed a necessary evil and an inevitable one, begotten by the remissnesse of the Political Body, and by the corruption of the Clergy. I do finde that two high injustices were the primitive causes thereof, the first was the usurpations of the *Saxons*, *Danes*, and *Normans*; the second was the peaceful humor and dispositions of King *James*, and the idlenesse and sloathfulnesse of the Nobility, who constrained their younger brethren to serve them, or to learn Trades, by taking away from them the means to subsist by the way of Arms; which is a priviledge more then legitimate, due by the elder brother to the younger, and by Princes to such Martial Spirits as live in their Dominions; if the *Saxons* and other Usurpers of Con-

See History and Policy reviewed.

Conquerors of *England* did by force of Arms become Masters of the Countrey, and did cast out the right Possessours thereof, and by success of time falling from a Forreign Injustice into a Domestick Injustice, they reduced their younger Brothers to Mecannick professions.

At present they demand that they may be permitted to expose their bloods and their lives for the preservation of their Brethrens : That the exercise of Arms may be abolished in so Populous and Warlike a State : that the banished glory which formerly with so much Pomp reigned in *England* may be restored again.

And as for the War which his late Highness declared against *Spain*, that is so generous, that a man may averre, that glory was the onely motive thereof, and that thereby he espoused the Interest of all the people which were oppressed, and of all the Princes which the Ambition of *Spain* had despoyled of their States and Territories. And the two most unfortunate people of the earth were the first objects of his Generosity, and those which were the most of all abandoned, were the first that felt the effects of that Arm which stretched it self forth to their assistance, To wit, the poor Indians, those wretched slaves, who behold no other faces save those of their tormentors ; and who were made to believe that perishing in the Mines of *Peru*, they thereby did raise to themselves Thrones of Glory in Heaven, since thereby they furnished *Spain* wherewithal to adorne and inrich Altars throughout the whole world. In these torrid

Which you may see in two Books, *viz.* Teats of the *Indies*, and the other, *America* Painted to the life.

Climates

Climates the gallant English went to revenge the death of several Merchants, and many brave Sea-men of all Nations, which the Spaniards did surprize in those Seas; and who they did decoy and attract by specious promises, that they would not mischief them : Notwithstanding the Law of Nations, and the Faith which they had plighted, they seized their ships, and having tyed the men alive to trees, placed this Superscription on their Breasts, *Who sent for you into this Countrey?* And let them there starve to death, whilest the Birds of the Air did feed upon their flesh as they were yet alive.

And also *Flanders*, the Sea whereof like unto a sharp humour, did alwayes nourish the wounds and incurable evils, she never was in so fair a way to recover her perfect health by the neighbourly refreshments which *England* at present doth profer unto her, and the fresh Air which *France* would also have her enjoy. Nor was the French letting her blood sufficient to cure her, for she needed an English Physician who was accustomed to cure and treat incurable bodies; so that in case this unfortunate fair one will in the least conform her self to those Remedies which are profered unto her, and the which will be no violenter then she her self pleaseth; she may be rendred plump and well liking, as the fresh Air and Blossoms of *France* can make her, and as the Sweets and Delicacies of *England* can procure unto her.

In like manner, it was a high point of Generosity

roſity in the Engliſh, ſince they cauſed *France* to loſe *Graveling* and *Dunkirk*, to help *France* again to re-take ſuch places in thoſe parts as might repay them with uſe, and elſewhere alſo, ſuch as might ſtand them in as great ſtead; as *Montmedy*, which was the firſt conſiderable reduced place after this happy Alliance, and the which crowned the ſame.

And truly here we may conſider the Generoſity of his late Highneſs, in its moſt perfect dye or luſter; for without having regard to thoſe Advantages which *Spain* might render him as to the Commerce, the places of Hoſtage which ſhe profered to put into his hands for ſecure Retreats, as *Graveling*, *Dunkirk*, and others; he was ſwayed by thoſe Reſentments which the Engliſh Nation ought to have harboured for the ſeveral and innumerable injuries and wrongs ſuſtained by that Nation; as the Spaniſh intended Invaſion with their great Fleet in 88. Their Tyranny in the Indies, and the Cruelties and Barbariſmes which they inflict upon all thoſe who will not acquieſs unto, and follow their Maximes and Opinions. His late Highneſs therefore preferred the Alliance and League with *France*, becauſe it was more Chriſtian-like, permitting all men to make uſe of that Liberty of Conſcience and Freedom, which Jeſus Chriſt hath acquired unto them by his Blood; and gaining them by meekneſs and courteouſneſs to his Divine example, and not by Cruelties and Oppreſſions.

His

His late Highness sided with *France*, the rather, because she hath undertaken the Defence of all oppressed people, as well Princes as Subjects. And to alledge all in one word, and so to compleat the height of Generosity it self, because *France* at that time was the weakest, as being abandoned by some of her ancient Allies, and as it were quite disordered by an intestine War, which had most violently shaken her bowels; so likewise must *France* needs confess, that without the assistance of *England*, her Navigation was totally ruined; the Pyrats of *Dunkirk* having blocked up all her Sea Ports, in so much, that Merchandizes were brought in as it were by stealth; and *France* might have been forced to have kept but a lean *Lent*, all their Farms and Farmers being destroyed; their Butter, Cheese, and all kinde of Spices and other Wares of that nature, being set at such rates as the Common people were not able to pay for them: So that had not the *English* scoured their Seas, and driven away and chased those Pyrats which lay lurking in such neighbouring Ports, *France* had been in a sad condition; whereas now by the means of the *English*, all Forreign Nations come freely into the French Ports with their Ships and Goods. And for to increase the courtesie of the *English* yet more to *France*, by saving the French the labour, charges, and hazzards of going to the Indies, they thence bring home unto their doors, in Exchange of their Linnen and Wines, all the good things and delicacies

cacies, which not onely the New World, but the reſt of the World plentifully and abundantly affords.

I ſhall enlarge my ſelf no further in theſe Political Reflections, but referre the Reader to the incomparable Work lately Printed, intituled, *Hiſtory and Policy reviewed.*

FINIS.

Courteous Reader,

These Books following, with others, are printed for Nath. Brook, *and are to be sold at his Shop at the* Angel *in* Cornhill.

V   7. The

7. The zealous Magiftrate; a Sermon by *T. Threfcot. Quarto.*

8. *Britannia Rediviva.* A Sermon before the Judges, *Auguft* 1648. by *J. Shaw* Minifter of *Hull.*

9. The Princefs Royal, in a Sermon before the Judges, *March* 24. by *J. Shaw.*

10. Judgement fet, and Books opened, Religion tried whether it be of God or Man, in feveral Sermons; by *J. Webfter. Quarto.*

11. Ifraels Redemption, or, the Prophetical Hiftory of our Saviours Kingdome on Earth; by *R. Matton.*

12. The Caufe and Cure of Ignorance, Error, and Profanenefs; or, a more hopeful way to Grace and Salvation; by *R. Young. Octavo.*

13. A Bridle for the Times, tending to ftill the murmuring, to fettle the wavering, to ftay the wandring, and to ftrengthen the fainting: by *J. Brinfley* of *Yarmouth.*

14. The fum of Practical Divinity: or, the grounds of Religion in a Chatechiftical way, by Mr. *Chriftopher Love* late Minifter of the Gofpel: a ufeful piece.

15. Heaven and Earth fhaken; a Treatife fhewing how Kings and Princes, their Governments are turned and changed, by *J. Davis* Minifter in *Dover*, admirably ufeful, and ferioufly to be confidered in thefe times.

16. The Treafure of the Soul; wherein we are taught, by dying to fin, to attain to the perfect love of God.

17. A Treatife of Contention, fit for thefe
fad

sad and troublesome times, by *J. Hall* Bishop of *Norwich.*

18. Select thoughts; or, choice helps for a pious spirit, beholding the excellency of her Lord Jesus: by *J. Hall* Bishop of *Norwich.*

19. The Holy Order , or Fraternity of Mourners in Zion; to which is added, Songs in the night, or chearfulness under afflictions: by *J. Hall* Bishop of *Norwich.*

23. The Celestial Lamp, enlightening every distressed Soul from the depth of everlasting darkness: by *T. Fetisplace.*

Admirable, and Learned Treatises of Occult Sciences in Philosophy, Magick, Astrology, Geomancy, Chymistry, Phisiognomy, and Chyromancy.

24. Magick and Astrology vindicated by *H. Warren.*

25. *Lux Veritatis*, Judicial Astrology vindicated and Demonology confuted; by *W. Ramsey,* Gent.

26. *Cornelius Agrippa* his fourth Book of Occult Philosophy, or Geomancy; Magical Elements of *Peter de Abona*, the nature of spirits: made English by *R. Turner.*

27. *Paracelsus* Occult Philosophy of the Mysteries of Nature and his secret Alchimy.

29. An Astrological Discourse with Mathematical Demonstrations; proving the influence of the Planets, and fixed Stars upon Elementary Bodies: by Sir *Christ. Heyden* Knight.

30. All Mr. *Lillies* Astrological Treatises collected into one Volume.

31. Ca

31. *Cataſtrophe Magnatum*: an Ephemerides for the Year 1652. by *N. Culpeper*.

32. *Teratologia*; or, a diſcovery of Gods Wonders, manifeſted by bloody Rain and Waters; by *J. S.*

34. Chyromancy; or the Art of divining by the Lines engraven in the hand of Man, by dame Nature, in 198. Genitures; with a Learned Diſcourſe of the Soul of the World: by *G. Wharton*, Eſq;

35. The Admired Piece of Phyſiognomy, and Chyromancy, Metopoſcopy, the Symmetrical Proportions, and Signal Moles of the Body, the Interpretation of Dreams; to which is added the Art of Memory, illuſtrated with Figures: by *Rich. Sanders*, in *Folio*.

36. The no leſs exquiſite then admirable Work, *Theatrum Chymicum. Britanicum*; containing ſeveral Poetical Pieces of our famous Engliſh Philoſophors, who have written the Hermitique Myſteries in their own ancient Language; faithfully collected into one Volume, with Annotations thereon: by the Indefatigable induſtry of *Elias Aſhmole*, Eſq; illuſtrated with Figures.

Excellent Treatiſes in the Mathematicks, Geometry, of Arithmetick, Surveying, and other Arts, or Mechanicks.

37. The incomparable Treatiſe of *Tactometria, ſeu Tetagmenometria*; or, the Gometry of Regulars, practically propoſed, after a new and

and moſt expeditious manner, together with the Natural or Vulgar, by way of Menſural comparison, and in the Solids, not onely in reſpect of Magnitude or Demenſion, but alſo of Gravity or Ponderoſity, according to any Metal aſſigned: together with uſeful experiments of Meaſures and Weights, obſervations on Gauging, uſeful for thoſe that are practiſed in the Art Metricald; by *T. Wybard.*

38. *Tectonicon*, ſhewing the exact meaſuring of all manner of Land, Squares, Timber, Stone, Steeples, Pillars, Globes; as alſo the making and uſe of the Carpenters Rule, &c. fit to be known by all Surveyors, Land-meters, Joyners Carpenters, and Maſons: by *L. Diggs.*

39. The unparallel'd Work for eaſe and expedition, intituled, The exact Surveyor: or, the whole Art of Surveying of Land, ſhewing how to plot all manner of Grounds, whether ſmall Incloſures, Champian, Plain, Wood-lands or Mountains, by the Plain Table; as alſo how to finde the Area, or Content of any Land, to Protect, Reduce or Divide the ſame; as alſo to take the Plot or Cart, to make a Map of any Mannor, whether according to *Rathburne*, or any other Eminent Surveyors Method; a Book excellently uſeful for thoſe that ſell, purchaſe, or are otherwiſe employed about Buildings; by *J. Eyre.*

40. The golden Treatiſe of Arithmetick, Natural and Artificial, or Decimals; the Theory and Practice united in a ſimpathetical Proportion, betwixt Lines and Numbers; in their

Quan-

Quantities and Qualities, as in respect of Form, Figure, Magnitude, and Affection ; demonstrated by Geometry, illustrated by Calculations, and confirmed with variety of Examples in every Species ; made compendious and easie for Merchants , Citizens , Sea-men. Accomptants, &c. by *Th.* Wilsford Corrector of the last Edition of *Record.*

41. Semigraphy, or the Art of Short-writing, as it hath been proved by many hundreds in the City of *London,* and other places, by them practised, and acknowledged to be the easiest, exactest, and swiftest method ; the meanest capacity by the help of this Book , with a few hours practice, may attain to a perfection in this Art ; by *J. Rich* Author and Teacher thereof, dwelling in *Swithins-Lane* in *London.*

42. Milk for Children ; a plain and easie Method teaching to read and write, useful for Schools and Families, by *J. Thomas* D. D.

43. The Painting of the Ancients ; the History of the beginning, progress, and consumating of the practice of that noble Art of Painting ; by *F. Junius.*

Excellent and approved Treatises in Physick, Chyrurgery, and other more familiar Experiments in Cookery, Preserving, &c.

44. *Culpeper's Semiatica Uranica,* his Astrological judgement of Diseases from the decumbiture of the sick, much enlarged : the way and manner of finding out the cause, change, and
end

end of the disease; also whether the sick be likely to live or die, and the time when Recovery or Death is to be expected, according to the judgement of *Hipocrates* and *Hermes Trismegistus*; to which is added Mr. *Culpepers* censure of Urines.

45. *Culpepers* last Legacy, left to his Wife for the publick good, being the choicest and most profitable of those secrets in Physick and Chyrurgery, which whilst he lived, were lockt up in his breast, and resolved never to be published till after his death.

46. The *York-shire* Spaw: or, the vertue and use of that water in curing of desperate diseases, with directions and rules necessary to be considered by all that repair thither.

47. The Art of Simpling: an introduction to the knowledge of gathering of Plants, wherein the difinitions, divisions, places, descriptions, differences, names, vertues, times of gathering, temperatures of them are compendiously discoursed of: also a discovery of the Lesser World, by *W. Coles*.

48. *Adam* in Eden, or Natures Paradise: the History of Plants, Herbs, and Flowers, with their several original names, the Places where they grow, their descriptions and kindes, their times of flourishing and decreasing; as also their several signatures, anatomical appropriations, and particular physical vertues; with necessary Observations on the Seasons of planting and gathering of our English Plants. A Work admirable useful for Apothecaries, Chyrurgeons,

and

and other Ingenuous perfons, who may in this Herbal finde comprized all the English phyfical Simples, that *Gerard* or *Parkinfon*, in their two voluminous Herbals have difcourfed of, even fo as to be on emergent occafions their own Phyficians, the ingredients being to be had in their own fields and gardens; Publifhed for the generall good, by *W. Coles*, M.D.

49. The Queens Clofet opened: incomparable Secrets in Phyfick, Chyrurgery, Preferving, Candying, and Cookery; as they were prefented to the Queen by the moft experienced perfons of our times; many whereof were honoured with her own Practice.

Elegant Treatifes in Humanity, Hiftory, Romances, and Poetry.

50. Times Treafury, or Academy for the accomplifhment of the English Gentry in Arguments of Difcourfe, Habit, Fafhion, Behaviour, &c. all fummed up in Characters of Honour, by *R. Brathwait* Efq.

51. *Oedipus*, or, the Refolver of the fecrets of Love, and other natural Problems, by way of Queftion and Anfwer.

52. The tears of the Indians: the Hiftory of the bloody and moft cruel proceedings of the Spaniards in the Ifland of *Hifpaniola, Cuba, Jamaica, Mexico, Peru*, and other places of the Weft-Indies; in which to the life are difcovered the tyrannies of the Spaniards, as alfo the juftnefs of our War fo fuccefsfully managed againft them.

53. The

52. The Illustrious Shepherdess. The Imperious Brother : written originally in Spanish by by that in comparable wit , *Don John Perez de Montalbans* ; translated at the requests of the Marchioness of *Dorchester*, and the Countess of *Stafford*, by *E. P.*

53. The History of the Golden Ass, as also the Loves of *Cupid* and his Mistress *Psiche* : by *L. Apulius* translated into English.

54. The Unfortunate Mother : a Tragedy by *T. N.*

55. The Rebellion : a Tragedy by *T. Rawlins.*

56. The Tragedy of *Messalina* the insatiate Roman Empress : by *N. Richards.*

57. The floating Island : a Trage-Comedy, acted before the King, by the Students of Christs-Church in *Oxon* ; by that renowned wit, *W. Strode*, the songs were set by Mr. *H Lawes.*

58. *Harvey*'s Divine Poems, the History of *Balaam*, of *Jonah*, and of St. *John* the Evangelist.

59. *Fons Lachrymarum*, or, a Fountain of tears ; the Lamentations of the Prophet *Jeremiah* in Verse, with an Elegy on Sir *Charles Lucas* : by *I. Quarles.*

60. Nocturnal Lucubrations, with other witty Epigrams and Epitaphs ; by *R. Chamberlain.*

Poetical, with several other accurately ingenuous Treatises, lately Printed.

62. Wits Interpreter , the English Parnassus : or a sure Guide to those admirable Accomplishments that compleat the English Gentry, in

in the most acceptable Qualifications of Discourse or Writing. An Art of Logick, accurate Complements, Fancies, Devices, and Experiments, Poems, Poetical Fictions, and *Al a mode* Letters : by *J. C.*

63 Wit and Drollery ; with other Jovial Poems : by Sir *J. M. M. L. M S. W. D.*

64. Sportive Wit, the Muses Merriment ; a new Spring of Drollery ; Jovial Fancies, &c.

65. The Admirable ingenuous Satyr against Hipocrites.

66. The Conveyancer of Light, or, the Compleat Clerk, and Scriveners Guide ; being an exact draught of all Presidents and Assurances now in use ; as they were penned, and perfected by diverse Learned Judges, Eminent Lawyers, and great Conveyancers, both Ancient and Modern : whereunto is added a Concordance from King *Richard* the 3. to this present.

67. *Themis Aurea*, The Laws of the Fraternity of the *Rosie Cross* ; in which, the occult Secrets of their Philosophical Notions are brought to light : written by *Count Mayerus*, and now Englisht by *T. H.*

68. The Iron Rod put into the Lord Protectors hand ; a Prophetical Treatise.

69 *Medicina Magica tamen Physica* ; Magical but Natural Physick : containing the general Cures of Infirmities and Diseases belonging to the Bodies of Men, as also to other animals and domestick Creatures, by way of Transplantion : with a Description of the most excellent Cordial out of Gold : by *Sam. Boulton* of *Salop.*

70. 7.

70. *J. Tradiscan's* Rareties, publisht by himself.

71. The Proceedings of the High Court of Justice against the late King *Charles,* with his Speech upon the Scaffold, and other proceedings, *Jan.* 30. 1648.

72. The perfect Cook : a right Method in the Art of Cookery, whether for Pastry, or all other manner of *Al a Mode* Kick-shaws ; with the most refined wayes of dressing flesh, fowl, or making of the most poinant Sawces, whether after the French, or English manner, with fifty five wayes of dressing of Eggs : by *M. M.*

73. The Expert Doctours Dispensatory : the whole Art of Physick restored to practice : the Apothecaries shop, & Chyrurgions Closet opened ; with a Survey, as also a correction of most Dispensatories now extant : with a Judicious Censure of their defects : and a supply of what they are deficient in : together with a learned account of the vertues and quantities, and uses of Simples and Compounds : with the Symptomes of Diseases : as also prescriptions for their several cures : by that renowned *P. Morellus,* Physician to the King of *France.*

74. Cabinet of Jewels, Mans Misery, Gods Mercy, Christs Treasury, &c. in eight excellent Sermons : with an Appendix of the nature of Tythes under the Gospel : with the expediency of Marriage in publique Assemblies, by *J. Crag.* Minister of the Gospel.

75. Natures Secrets : or the admirable and wonderful History of the generation of Meteors : descri-

describing the Temperatures of the Elements, the heights, magnitudes, and influences of Stars, the causes of Comets, Earthquakes, Deluges, Epidemical Diseases, and Prodigies of Precedent times : with presages of the weather : and descriptions of the weather-glass : by *T. Wilsford.*

76. The Mysteries of Love and Eloquence; or, the Arts of Wooing and Complementing; as they are managed in the *Spring Garden, Hide Park, the New Exchange,* and other eminent places : A work, in which are drawn to the life the Deportments of the most Accomplisht Persons : the Mode of their Courtly entertainments, Treatment of their Ladies at Balls, their accustomed Sports, Drolls and Fancies, the Witchcrafts of their perswasive Language, in their Approaches, or other more *Secret Dispatches,* &c. by *E. P.*

77. *Helmont* disguised : or, the vulgar errours of impercial and unskilful Practicers of Physick confuted : more especially as they concern the Cures of Feavers, the Stone, the Plague, and some other Diseases by way of Dialogue, in which the chief rareties of Physick are admirably discoursed of, by *I. T.*

Books very lately Printed, and in the Press now Printing.

1. THe Scales of Commerce and Trade : by *T. Wilsford.*
2. Geometry demonstrated by Lines and Num-

Numbers: from thence, Astronomy, Cosmography, and Navigation proved and delineated by the Doctrine of Plain and Spherical Triangles: by *T. Wilsford.*

3. The English Annals, from the Invasion made by *Julius Cesar* to these times: by *T. Wilsford.*

4. The Fool transformed: A Comedy.

5. The History of *Lewis* the eleventh King of *France*: a Trage-Comedy.

6. The Chaste woman against her will; a Comedy.

7. The Tooth-drawer, a Comedy.

8. Honour in the end: a Comedy.

9. Tell-tale: a Comedy.

10. The History of *Donquixiot*, or the Knight or the ill-favoured face; a Comedy.

11. The fair Spanish Captive: a Trage-Comedy.

12. Sir *Kenelm Digby*, and other persons of Honour, their rare and incomparable secrets of Physick, Chyrurgery, Cookery, Preserving, Conserving, Candying, distilling of Waters, extraction of Oyls, compounding of the costliest Perfumes, with other admirable Inventions and select Experiments, as they offered themselves to their Observations: whether here, or in forreign Countreys.

13. The Saints Tomb-stone: or, the Remains of the blessed. A plain Narrative of some markable Passages, in the holy Life, and happy Death of Mrs. *Dorothy Shaw*, Wife of Mr. *John Shaw*, Preacher of the Gospel at *Kingston* upon *Hull*, collected by her dearest Friends, especially
ly

ly for her sorrowful husband, and six Daughters
consolation and invitation.

14. Letters the most exquisite that are in any
Language, by Mr. *Robert Loveday*, who was the
late admired Translator of the Volumes of the
famed Romance Cleopatra, Published by his
dear Brother Mr. *A: L.*

15. The so long expected Work, the *New
World* of *English* Words, or, a general *Dictio-
nary*, containing the Terms, Etymologies, Defi-
nitions, and perfect Interpretations of the proper signification of hard *English* words throughout the Arts and Sciences, Liberal, or Mecha-
nick; as also other subjects that are useful, or
appertain to the Language of our Nation: to
which is added the signification of Proper
Names, Mythology, and Poetical Fictions, Historical Relations, Geographical Descriptions
of the Countreys, and Cities of the World: especially of these three Nations, wherein their
chiefest Antiquities, Battels, and other most memorable Passages are mentioned: by *E. P.*

16 A learned Comentary, on Psalm the fifteenth, by that Reverend and Eminent Divine
Mr. *Christopher Cartwright*, Minister of the Gospel in *York*, to which is prefixed a brief account
to the Authors life, and of his Work, by *R.
Bolton.*

17. The way to Bliss, in three Books, being
a learned Treatise of the Philosophers Stone,
made publique by *Elias Ashmole* Esq;

18. Wit restored in several Select Poems, not
formerly publisht by Sir *John Mennis*, Mr. *Smith*
and others.   19. The

19. The Modern Affurancer, the Clerks Directory, containing the Practick Part of the Law, in the exact Forms and Draughts of all manner of Prefidents for Bargains, and Sales, Grants, Feoffements, Bonds, Bills, Conditions, Covenants, Jointures, Indentures, &c. And all other Inftruments and Affurances now in ufe, by *John Hern.*

20. Naps upon Parnaffus. A fleepy Mufe nipt and pincht, though not awakened. Such voluntary and Jovial Coppies of Verfes as were lately received from fome of the W I T S of the Univerfities, in a Frolick : dedicated to *Gondibert's* Miftrefs, by Captain *Jones* and others, &c.

21. The compleat Midwife's Practice, in the high and weighty Concerments of Mankinde : the fecond Edition corrected and enlarged, with a full Supply of fuch moft ufeful and admirable Secrets which Mr. *Nicholas Culpeper* in his brief Treatife, and other Englifh Writers in the Art of Midwifry, have hitherto wilfully paffed by, kept cofe to themfelves, or wholly omitted : by *T. Chamberlaine,* M. P.

22. *America* Painted to the Life, the Hiftory of the Conqueft, and firft Original undertakings of the advancement of the Plantations in thofe Parts : with an exquifite Map, by *F. Gorges*, Efquire.

23. *Culpeper's* School of Phyfick, or the Experimental Practice of the whole Art ; fo reduced, either into Aphorifmes, or choice and tried Receipts, that the free-born Students of the three Kingdoms, may in this Method, finde

per-

perfect wayes for the operation of such Medicines, so astrologically and Physically prescribed, as that they may themselves be competent judges of the Cures of their Patients: by *N.C.*

24. *Blagrave's* admirable Ephemerides for the Year 1659.

25. History and Policy Reviewed in the Heroick transactions of his most Serene Highness, *Oliver* late Lord Protector, declaring his steps to Princely Perfection drawn in lively Parallels to the Ascents of the great Patriarch *Moses* to the height of 30 degrees of Honor, by *H. D. Esq.*

26. *J. Cleaveland* Revived: *Poems, Orations, Epistles,* and other of his Genuine Incomparable Pieces never before Publisht.

27. *England's* Worthies, Select Lives of the most eminent Persons of the three Nations *from Constantine* the Great, to these times: by *W. Winstanly.*

28. The History of the Life and Death of his most Serene Highness, *Oliver,* late Lord Protector. Wherein, from his Cradle to his Tomb, are impartially transmitted to Posterity, the most weighty Transactions, forreign or Domestique, that have happened in his Time, either in Matters of Law, Proceedings in Parliaments, or others Affairs in Church or State, by *S. Carrington.*

29. The right Lozenges publickly sold by *Edmund Buckworth* in St. *Katherines Court,* for Coughs, and Consumption of the Lungs, &c. are to be had at *Nath. Brook's* and *John Grismond's* in *Ivy-lane,* and at no other place.

FINIS.

CPSIA information can be obtained
at www.ICGtesting.com
Printed in the USA
BVHW081530230819
556642BV00022B/2552/P